" To _foc_____ S____t...
    To _____
  the f_____
  women I _Love_...

To: _Justin French AKA "Frenchy"_

From: _Dan, the man with_
              the plan...

THE WHOLE HEART OF

THE COMPLETE TEACHINGS FROM THE ORAL TRADITION OF LAO-TZU

The Whole Heart of™ *Tao*
Copyright © 2006 by Fey Family Wu-Su, Inc.
New Forest® is a registered trademark of Fey Family Wu-Su, Inc.
Book design by Pat Covert
Calligraphy by Rev. John A. Bright-Fey

"The Whole Heart of" is a trademark of Crane Hill Publishers,
Inc.

ISBN-13: 978-1-57587-247-6
ISBN-10: 1-57587-247-1

Published by Crane Hill Publishers
www.cranehill.com

Printed in China

Library of Congress Cataloging-in-Publication Data

Bright-Fey, J. (John)
    The whole heart of Tao / By John Bright-Fey.
      p. cm.
    ISBN-13: 978-1-57587-247-6
    1. Tao. 2. Philosophy, Taoist. 3. Mind and body.   I.
Title.
  B127.T3B75 2006
  181'.114–dc22

2006004872

THE WHOLE HEART OF

TAO

THE COMPLETE TEACHINGS FROM THE ORAL TRADITION OF LAO-TZU

REVEREND VENERABLE
JOHN BRIGHT-FEY

CRANE HILL
PUBLISHERS

TAO: THE WAY

DEDICATION AND ACKNOWLEDGMENTS

This book brings to light the heretofore-secret oral literature of ancient China. It seems only fitting that those individuals who kept the tradition alive be acknowledged for their efforts. Therefore, I dedicate this book to the Dharma Mind Seal Lineage Holders of the Blue Dragon Order of Esoteric Zen Buddhism. These individuals devoted themselves to the preservation of the old in the ever-changing face of the new.

Kwan Ng Lo (1524 - ?): Founder/Warrior/Innocent
P'ang Ben Yu
P'ang Shih Yu
Ma Tin Hwa
Sung Nin Jan
Meng Cho Yao
Fei Tzu Lin
Sun Lok
Lo Ng Gao
Sun Ma Hao
Chi Wing Chow

John Bright-Fey: Current Lineage Holder

Thank you for reminding us that we stand on the shoulders of giants.

TABLE OF CONTENTS

INTRODUCTION

The Tao Te Ching is the fundamental text of both philosophic and religious Taoism. It was written during the Spring and Autumn Classical Period (700–480 BCE) by a native of the southern Chinese feudal state of Ch'u named Li Erh. According to legend, Li Erh, an imperial librarian, keenly observed the world around him, including the political intrigues of China's feudal lords. He recorded what he saw and employed ancient Shamanic rituals as a means of understanding the complexities of human interaction. Eventually, he distilled his lifetime of knowledge into a long poem written in the literary language of the period. This poem is the Tao Te Ching. Because it was filled with both ancient wisdom and the profound insight of a child, Li Erh became known as Lao-tzu, which combines the meanings of "old wise man" and "innocent child." Since then, Taoist mystics have referred to Lao-tzu as "The Ancient Child."

11

THE TAO TE CHING:
THE SOURCE AND ITS EFFECTS

The poem known as the Tao Te Ching *is composed of roughly 5,000 ancient Chinese characters arranged in archaic poetic form and rhyme scheme. Its language is at once cryptic, terse, and very beautiful and eloquent. Supposedly, it reflects the personality of Lao-tzu himself. In fact, many Taoists often refer to the poem simply as "The Lao-tzu." It describes the source of all life and existence (Tao) and the benevolent effects (Te) that the all-pervading source has on mankind. The poem itself is a complete classic body (ching) of Chinese wisdom that has been studied by scholars for centuries. It stands as one of the most popular works in all of the world's great literature.*

While there are many translations of the Tao Te Ching *available, most of them simply deliver the cargo; that is to say, each accomplishes the task of translation with great care and smooth efficiency. However, the academic professionalism of the translator often gets between the reader and what is being read. This is an unavoidable consequence of translation from one language to another. Invariably, the personality and life experience of the translator will be reflected in the translation. While each of the available* Tao Te Ching *translations in English is wonderful in its own way, none of them adequately reflects the perspective of a practicing Taoist that has been initiated into the mystic tradition—that is, until now.*

Traditionally, the poetry and information presented in this edition are passed down orally from Master to student as part of a deep initiation into the Taoist mysteries. It is called a "Direct Transmission Of The Way." Memorization, meditation, and feedback in the form of Chinese mystic calligraphy are vital parts of the process.

The Direct Transmission of the Tao Te Ching *is somewhat difficult to understand from a western context. It would be similar to memorizing the complete Gospels of Matthew, Mark, Luke, and John, deeply contemplating select passages, and rendering them into an illuminated manuscript. Your experience would be judged by the quality and artistic detail of the manuscript itself, as well as the prayerful behavior manifested by a Christian-based mystic encounter.*

The Tao Te Ching *you are about to read comes from the secret oral tradition of the T'ien-Shih, or "Celestial Masters," sect of Taoism that combines elements of both the philosophic and religious schools. Also known as the Wu-tou-mi Tao (Five Pecks of Rice School), this sect maintains a private body of arcane Taoist rituals, meditation techniques, and mystic literature. Initiates in this school are charged with maintaining a continuous link with Lao-tzu himself in order that authentic Taoist wisdom of the past will always be available in the present. It is this wisdom that I want to share with you.*

ON THIS TRANSLATION

There is no direct way to substitute one English word for a single Chinese character. Instead, characters can represent many English words and concepts. The ancient Chinese language of the Tao Te Ching is a particularly complex and nuanced one that abounds with paradox. Additionally, a Chinese character has a depth of meaning with many subsidiary meanings "beneath" its predominant one. This is true of the English language as well, but few of us are aware of it on a day-to-day basis. The language of the Tao Te Ching is context-oriented, wherein one of the character's minor meanings becomes the major, depending on what other characters are around it. This overlaps with Chinese poetic form and rhyme scheme, which allows for multiple interpretations of a block of characters. In essence, deliberate visual enjambment is presented to the reader throughout the text. This would be akin to reading a paragraph in English not from the beginning to the end, but from the middle outward in a nonlinear way guided by a unique combination of literary knowledge and intuition.

Ancient Chinese is a complex literary language that employs phrases, images, and words, as it were, from older works of literature, poetry, and philosophy. To get an idea of what this means, think of writing a letter to a complete stranger employing only lines from the plays of William Shakespeare. Your skill at communicating a concrete idea, such as your decision to move to a new city, would depend entirely upon choosing just the right lines and arranging them on the page in just the right order. The stranger's skill at interpreting the lines would also be an important part of the equation. If you add a mystical element to the endeavor, wherein the reader of the letter must engineer a specific mood and altered state of consciousness to understand it, then you will begin to grasp the idea of the Tao Te Ching's archaic language.

For this translation, I have chosen to exclude capital letters and used English punctuation only sparingly, since ancient Chinese contains neither. I have employed several neologisms that support authentic Taoist thinking. For example, the single word "bodymind" is intended to convey a deeper meaning than its constituent parts. Popular culture abounds with talk of reuniting the body with the mind. Taoist Cultivators, however, see no such separation to be remedied. That the body and mind form a unity is a foregone conclusion.

Normal use of grammatical voice, tense, and gender is problematic where the oral tradition is concerned. I have tried to reflect the intent and feel of the spoken verse as it exists in the Taoist tradition. Whenever possible, I adhered to the same usage in my comments.

The choices of poetic structure are my own and reflect the long hours of recitation necessary to memorize the Tao Te Ching. They are also my attempts to translate ancient Chinese poetic forms into a contemporarily relevant structure for English readers.

I believe the world at large could benefit greatly from the authentic wisdom and knowledge contained in the

Tao Te Ching. *Yet so much of the conventional information about it obscures more than it reveals. I humbly offer my own translation as a potential remedy to this situation. Now you will be able to journey into the Taoist heart and soul.*

Let not your heartmind be troubled
Simply
Flow into the Tao.

—John Bright-Fey, Taoist Master
Reverend Venerable, Tao-jen, Tao-shih

(verbal or Written Communication)

THE DIRECT TRANSMISSION OF THE TAO TE CHING

What follows is the poetic record of a journey into the Taoist heart and soul. It occurred, as it has for thousands of years, during the direct transmission of the 5,000 Character Classic of the Ancient Child, known to the world more commonly as Lao-tzu's *Tao Te Ching*.

Once you have experienced a direct transmission—especially in the Taoist tradition—all other methods of learning seem mundane or pedestrian. It is a profound experience that is engineered within a highly ritualized environment, replete with invocations, stylized physical activity, artistic brush writing, complex discourse, and arcane meditations. During the transmission, the Master and student (the sender and receiver, respectively) experience a shared consciousness infused with deep meaning and cascades of metaphysical nuance. It is among the most life altering of all earthly events. Upon completion, not only is the text itself transmitted, but a vast mystical subtext is successfully embedded into the bodymind of the student who then becomes the next living link in a chain that stretches back for millennia.

This way of learning is a guided eduction. "Educe" means to "draw out," and that is exactly what occurs during a direct transmission. To the Taoist way of thinking, all the knowledge of the universe is locked away inside each of us. The transmission of the *Tao Te Ching* begins to unlock that wisdom and knowledge.

While the student is learning how to physically write each of the 5,000+ Chinese characters of the text, he is instructed in the history of their evolution and etymology via verbal and written instructions. Artistic detail, as well as the history and development of these graphic building blocks, is also transmitted to the student. At the same time, he is instructed in specific meditation and visualization techniques that begin to alter his experience of the characters' rendering.

The Master will stop the student during his writing and ask very specific questions regarding physical sensations, emotional reactions to the transmission process, and even recollections of past dreams and imaginings. The Master will palpate specific energy loci on the student's bodymind. Like a doctor of Traditional Chinese Medicine, he will read the pulse, test muscular strength, carefully observe the breathing of the student, and judge the student's level of engagement in the process by observing changes in tonal inflection when conversing. Even the strength of breath behind the student's spoken words is a vital indicator of the direct transmission process.

Periodically during the transmission, the Master instructs the student in specific *qigong* (life-force yoga) activities designed to support and actualize the entire event. Some of the techniques take several moments to perform, while others take hours or more.

This is a trans-conscious experience in which the student is gently guided by the Master into an altered state of perception in which the profound non-ordinary wisdom of the unconscious mind is educed, that is, drawn out into ordinary waking perception. The depth and authenticity of the mystic state is judged by the Master in primarily three ways: by the trained observance of changes in the complex energetic physiology of the student; the quality and dynamics of the actual Chinese characters themselves rendered with brush and ink on paper; and through the creation of root verse that accurately reflects a bodymind mystically entrenched in the ancient Taoist memory.

Root verse, or core verse, is a blend of esoteric and academic translation, paraphrase, and original spontaneous poetry in which the student is able to disengage the logical discriminatory mind and allow non-ordinary wisdom to flow out of the unconscious mind. It is an act of literary surrender to the poetic moment so total that the receiver of the direct transmission is fundamentally altered forever.

Contained within the root verse are the Taoist secrets of breath mastery, internal alchemic transformation, yogic cultivation, and inspired living. Likewise, the keys to decoding Chinese esoteric language and symbolism are revealed to the student, who, under the watchful eye of the Master, becomes the artistic player in a revealed vision that will guide him through the time bound into the timeless.

This is the seminal experience in the life of a Taoist Mystic, which once enjoined forever alters his world view. The most important thing to me, however, is that the entire affair is accomplished through the agency of poetry.

Before proceeding to the translation itself, I will provide a brief description of the actual direct transmission process written as a kind of "play in one act." This will give you a glimpse into the heretofore-secret world of Taoist mystic initiation. Following this description will be my original translation and commentary of the classic itself.

THE TEXT AND COMMENTARY

Among Taoist mystics who have received transmission of the 5,000 Character Classic in this way, it is common to receive this teaching only once in a lifetime. I was fortunate enough to receive it a total of three times from two different Taoist Masters. The first experience was exciting and profound, while the successive transmissions were exponentially breathtaking and quite beyond conceptual expression. They were also very private experiences. Yet, I want to share a portion of them with you.

This presentation of the *Tao Te Ching* will be accompanied by an exposition into its dynamics. The commentary that follows each of the eighty-one chapters will explain the inner workings of each stanza. These have been numbered for convenient reference. The comments themselves will be classified in one or more of four ways:

The Taoist Mind: This reflects the proper mindset and world view of the traditional Taoist. Specifically, these comments outline precisely how a Taoist thinks.

The Taoist Body: These comments will address the day-to-day concerns of the Taoist, or how the Taoist lives his life.

The Taoist Hand: Comments under this heading concern the actual training techniques employed by a Cultivator of the Tao. These techniques establish the spiritual discipline of the Taoist.

The Taoist Heart: Comments under this heading reflect Taoist core beliefs. More simply put, these are the things that a Taoist holds dear.

Frequently, my comments will cover facets of two or more of these classifications. Overlapping concerns and principles abound in many of the world's great philosophical traditions, and Taoism is no different.

A GLIMPSE OF THE TAOIST DIRECT TRANSMISSION

Play In One Act

Scene: A room of approximately 400 square feet adjacent to a large open area that serves as a training hall for the practice of traditional *T'ai Chi Ch'uan* and similar arts. The room itself is south-facing as determined by the science of Feng-shui, or geomancy. On the north wall is a shrine dedicated not to any deity or personage, but to the concept of perpetual change. A single large Chinese character written in cursive style forms the framed centerpiece of the shrine. Flowers, candles, and incense censer adorn the shrine. In front of it is a place for seated meditation, replete with cushions and a folded wool blanket. To the right of the shrine is a calligraphy table that has been constructed specifically for this transmission. It is a flat surface approximately waist high and is decorated with esoteric Chinese characters and an intersecting pattern of lines that seemingly divide the table into quadrants. On the table is paper roughly eighteen inches wide from a continuous roll, several ink stones and ink sticks for hand-grinding calligraphy ink, several small bowls for collecting the ink, and a teapot filled with fresh spring water. A series of antique Chinese paperweights hold the paper in place. There is a smaller square table to the right of the main calligraphy table that is specifically designed to hold a one-and-a-half-inch layer of red sand on its surface. A small scorched branch of peach-wood eight inches long lies on top of the sandy layer. Both of these tables are sufficient distance from the walls and each other to allow an unobstructed walkway around them. A single chair rests against the facing wall, which supports a series of elegantly framed and very old Chinese calligraphy.

Both the Master/transmitter and student/receiver are clothed in loose-fitting, brightly colored ceremonial garb decorated with Taoist symbols, star constellations, and embroidered versions of Chinese characters.

Appropriate ablutions having been performed, an hour-long session of hand grinding calligraphy ink commences. This will be the ink used for drawing the characters. This grinding is performed as a mindfulness meditation.

The specific line of characters to be transmitted is comprised of only four characters. These four characters form what is commonly referred to as the first line of the twenty-sixth chapter of the *Tao Te Ching*. (Author's Note: Within the Taoist mystic tradition, no established delineation of chapters is universally recognized. Classically, from this perspective, the 5,000 Character Classic is one long continuous poem without chapters or sections. Historically, these divisions have been imposed upon it in a variety of arrangements for a variety of reasons.) These four characters can be academically translated in a number of ways: "Being heavy is the root of being light" or "That which is heavy is that which is light." Most of the standard translations involve some permutation of the interplay between the concepts of heaviness, lightness, root, stability, or inside and outside. However, none of the standard translations are mystic translations borne out of the process of direct transmission within the Taoist tradition. Consequently, the authentic meaning of the four characters is lost as are the instructions in Taoist bodymind cultivation.

The Master and student face each other and the transmission begins:

MASTER: The question is one of the source, and the source is one of questioning.

STUDENT: Could you please be more specific?

MASTER: No. As with all Taoism, intuition is the only path to understanding.

STUDENT: And this intuition is not completely free, is it?

MASTER: That is correct. This intuition is a guided search and guided finding. Complete freedom is a dead end.

Standing meditation is then performed upon the concept of freedom and the shape of the bodymind. This standing can take place for more than an hour if the Master so determines.

MASTER: Where can you find the source in your bodymind? Where you can you find the power in your bodymind?

STUDENT: They can be found in a joining.

MASTER: A joining of what?

STUDENT: A joining of anything in space and time.

MASTER: Show me the source and power by joining these two exercises.

Instruction in two qigong, or Chinese yoga, activities takes place, alternating one and then the other in a continuous series. Each one is short and done in a standing posture. Each time the student moves one to the other, he says, "I am the source; I am the power." The teacher adjusts the student's postures, and the student continues. Approximately fifteen to nineteen minutes elapse. The student perceives a point of bright white light in his visual field. The student relays this to the teacher.

MASTER: Is this light inside or outside of you?

STUDENT: There is no inside or outside. Both are the same.

MASTER: Close your eyes and continue the *qigong*. First, please, rephrase my question.
(The tone in the Master's voice is somewhat angry and is meant to play upon the student's emotions. The emotional response is designed to adjust the energetic connection that the student has with the earth. The student experiences his legs filling with *qi*, or life-force energy. Immediately thereafter, he experiences a wiggling sensation in his thighs and the bottoms of his feet.)

STUDENT: My thinking is clearing. (Pause)

STUDENT: But where is it? Where can you find the connection?

MASTER: Excellent. But what is the connection? Answer only in a questioning tone.

STUDENT: Is it a moment? Is it a moment that can be grasped?

The Master puts his left hand on the student's lower abdomen and his right hand on the student's mid-back and presses in slightly. He pushes in quickly, as if to force out some of the student's air.

MASTER: Answer your question. Compose verse, please.

STUDENT: Yes.
It can be grasped.
Let me show you how to listen to immortality.
Because now I can hear it.

MASTER: How does it sound?

STUDENT: It sounds like the bright light.

MASTER: The bright light you hear is the name of Lao-tzu. You are almost ready to see the characters.

First, however, what tri-gram seems to hold the most wisdom for you at this very moment?

The Master then points to a painting hanging on the wall that contains a series of eight tri-grams known as the Pa Kua. These are ancient Chinese symbols used to categorize different phases of human experience.

STUDENT: *Sun* is the name of the tri-gram. It has two expressive lines and one receptive.

MASTER: Good! Now maintain a light and sensitive energy at the top of your head as I show you how to form the next four characters in the Classic.

The Master then begins to gesture in the air in front of the student. The paths of his movements are obviously the strokes that would form the four characters in this line, but they are also the movements from Taoist ritual dance. At the end of his physical performance, he vocalizes the sound—

MASTER: "Tzu"—
—as a long, drawn-out exhalation.
The sound must be made before and after each character.

Now instructions in the actual stroke order and shape of the character take place. As the student writes them, the Master comments on their formation and structure. The "Tzu" sound is reverberating throughout the room.

After the four characters are learned, the Master then tells the student to study them carefully. A long period of silence goes by as the student focuses in on the four characters.

MASTER: Root verse, please! Compose! Write! Put it in the form of a question. There is only energy in the question.

STUDENT: but where can you find the connection
it is a bright moment that can be grasped
tzu gravity intelligence must have a center
to find its core
and bring auspicious stability
to those quarters shallow
and not yet complete

as foundation and embodied root
tzu gravity intelligence
secures profundity in the un-profound
for the planet on which we stand and its wonders
is both our model and our entry point
to this concentration of impervious integrity

That ends the Direct Transmission of the first four characters of Chapter Twenty-six of the *Tao Te Ching*. In this translation, these first four characters correspond with the first five stanzas.

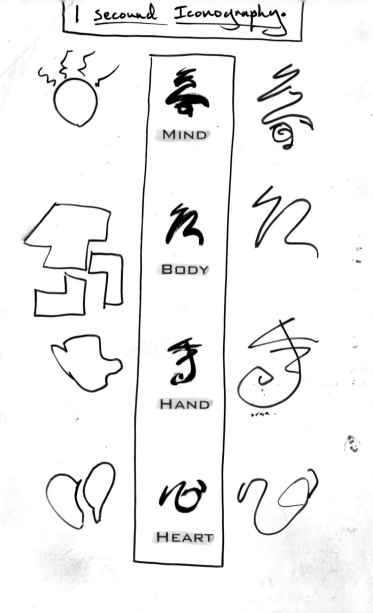

1 secound Iconography.

MIND

BODY

HAND

HEART

Mind / Body / Hand / Heart

[Hand] is our personal Interaction
with our Environment / Surroundings.

CHAPTER ONE

1 the _tao_ source of life that we often talk about
is beyond the power of words and labels to
        define or enclose

2 while it is true that we employ words and labels
        to outline our
experience
they are not absolute and cannot define the absolute

3 when it all began there were no words or labels

4 these things were created out of the union of
        preception and
perception •••••

5 whether a person who is awake in play
sees the heart of life or its surface manifestations is
        hardly
important
because they are exactly the same point in space
and time

31

6 the words and labels that we use make us think that
    they are
different
but only so we can talk about it from the outside of
    ourselves
in regard to the outside of the point in space and time

7 if you feel as though you really need a name
then call it the wonderwork
and watch one miracle talk to another
in a language that you can feel but not understand

8 it is playful to approach something that is logically
unknowable

Justin: Writing helps me remember on learn.

COMMENTARY

The first chapter of the Tao Te Ching *establishes the
philosophical stance of a Taoist Cultivator. It also contains
instructions for the fundamental meditative technique that
has been employed by Taoists for millennia.*

*According to oral tradition, Lao-tzu employed ancient
ritual and meditative techniques to nourish his mind and
body, to refine his spirit, and to cultivate a profound
sense of the world around him. Early on, he was*

confronted by many difficulties. As his awareness increased, however, it allowed him to eventually penetrate the world of illusions and glimpse the ultimate reality of life. Lao-tzu employed a single word as a convenient label for this ultimate reality: Tao.

1-2 HEART: These stanzas state plainly that the words that we use to describe the Tao are completely inadequate and, on some level, can't be trusted. Taoists are keenly aware that words affect a person's physiology. Specific words you use and how you employ them can color your experience of what you come in contact with during your life ③ neurology

3 HEART: Before the differentiating mind of a human being develops, things are experienced directly. It's a state of pre-language, a pre-awareness before our ② neurology convinces us that there's an outside reality and an inside reality and that there is a separation between the two. The philosophy of the *Tao Te Ching* begins at the point where we realize that much of what we assume about these inside and outside worlds isn't really true at all, but is just a trick of our neurology.

4 MIND: Your organs of preception (your senses) combine and join with your organ of perception (your brain) to create a picture of what you experience. Much of what you experience is ① tangible. Yet the self that is doing the experiencing remains ① intangible.

① Tangible / Intangible

33

5 MIND: Awake in play can best be described by comparing it to the rapt attention of a child who is completely engaged in what he or she is doing. Adults don't have a clue what's going on inside a child's mind when a stick becomes a fiery horse or Excalibur. But the child's mind sees a panorama of things, and his play is real, it's visceral and authentic. It has a profound effect on the entire bodymind.

To a Taoist, it isn't necessary at that moment when engaged in play to penetrate to the very core/heart/answer/center of the mystery or to dance around the surface of it, because none of it actually reveals the Tao Source; it just allows the Taoist access to the ultimate reality of the Source.

Imagination is our Source of Reality.

6 HEART and MIND: Words, labels, and constructs are necessary to outline the Tao Source. Taoists do not decry the workings of the central nervous system and the mind that differentiates. Rather, they embrace the central nervous system and the mind that differentiates without giving it total control over them. Your bodymind provides a laboratory by which you can explore the universe and a crucible by which you can refine its essence. This is fundamental: Taoism is an experiential—not a theoretical—philosophy. If quantum physics is the physics of possibility, then the Taoist lifestyle is the total experience of possibility.

7 HAND: These are instructions for the fundamental Taoist meditative technique. Simply put, the Cultivator places himself in a state of complete reflection where he is just watching and observing an event in spacetime. The goal of this basic Taoist meditative technique is to become the Transcendental Witness. To be a Transcendental Witness is to acknowledge the indeterminate nature of the vastness of one's self. A Transcendental Witness sees everything, or just one thing, or everything in one thing, all at the same time. But the goal is always the same. The Transcendental Witness in a state of complete and total reflection observes so that they may uncover clues to the Tao Source and Way of Life.

8 MIND and BODY: The final stanza of this chapter is a gentle injunction to remain playful and childlike in all of your Taoist pursuits. You must remain playful because you're approaching something that cannot possibly be conquered with the intellect. In Taoist parlance, if you are able to conquer a facet of the *Tao* with your intellect, then you were not looking at the true *Tao*. Within the Taoist context, playfulness is complete engagement and complete engagement yields authenticity. Taoists regard something playful as something authentic and vice versa.

Visceral or Authentic.

related" to deep Inward feelings/ not Intellect

35

"Real or not Fake.

positive / Negative = ☯

CHAPTER TWO

1   as a matter of course

2   if you decide that something is beautiful
    then something else immediately becomes ugly
    without you realizing it

3   if you enter a thought shape that dictates the
            parameters of
    what is a condition of health
    then the parameters of a condition of unhealthy
    come forward

4   you create death when you decide what constitutes
            life
    you create difficulties when you create ease
    you create long when you decide what is short
    you create a low tone when you sing a high one

5   were you aware of the power of your own lifeforce

6   when looking to the left
    different tones create harmony

7   whether you are truly clever or merely awake
    manage your affairs without actions
    and rely on fluid thinking rather than stagnant
     thought

8   adapt to conditions that present themselves
    and remember that specialization
    is not the useful way

9   continuously create instead of acquiring
    and enjoy what you create

10 you are important only if it is not important to you

COMMENTARY

1 **MIND:** This stanza begins a discussion of the discriminating mind, which is the mind that generates the illusion of our separateness from the wonders of the Tao Source and Way of Life. Lao-tzu recognized that the subtle inner workings of our neurology falsely render our experience of life as something that occurs outside of our bodymind. The phrase "as a matter of course" also implies the inevitability of group-think or consensus reality and how the actions and behaviors

of others around you also contribute to this illusion of separateness.

2-4 HEART and MIND: The Taoist mindset holds that we are active participants in our experience of the world around us, and we must be aware of that fact. That we enter thoughts and wear them like a coat is a core Taoist belief. These thoughts-as-things shape and change our bodyminds to fit the reality that they represent. They affect us even to the point of reorganizing our biology. This ability is, fundamentally, a creative act in which we don't so much believe what we see as much as we see what we already believe. This result is a differentiated experience of the world in which we look at things through the lens of conflict and opposition. To learn how to step back from this dynamic and witness the inner workings of the bodymind is a core Taoist practice and is fundamental to Taoist meditation.

5 HEART and HAND: Life-force energy, or *qi*, is the agent of change. The tone of this stanza is questioning. This is a self-reflective meditative technique in which the Taoist sits quietly, asks the question of himself, and bathes in the interrogative.

6 HAND: This refers to the intuition. Engaging the intuitive mind through meditation and learning to hear it is of primary importance to the Cultivator, because it is through the intuition that the *Tao* speaks to the

Taoist. Your intuition must run the show, so to speak, if a harmonious life is to be led.

7 BODY and HAND: "Truly clever" refers to the intellect while "merely awake" refers to the illuminated mind. To manage without actions is, among other things, an injunction to avoid purposefully imposing too many rules on one's behavior.

8 BODY: Live a relaxed lifestyle that changes and adapts to whatever life throws at you. Specialization in this case refers to becoming habitual in only one way of living and reacting to life.

9 BODY: These are Taoist life instructions.

10 MIND: Regard all Taoist cultivation as the single most important thing in the universe—your very survival depends on it—while at the same time holding it casually, almost to the point of disregarding it altogether.

CHAPTER THREE

1 be wary of exalting the wise and sophisticated
for it becomes not unlike
pouring two liquids into a container meant for one

2 consider the relative wisdom of displaying
treasures
that remain untouched in temporary keeping

3 authentic learning released through insight
nurtures the heart spirit
and does not disturb the balance

4 a sound leader helps the populace to be open
minded and self
aware

5 with open heart spirits
strong bodyminds
even temperaments and thought clarity

Handwritten annotations:
nurtures the Heart Spirit
Take the time to understand

40

6   these people make their own choices
and can naturally resist those meddling fools who
     try to steal their
ability
to respond

7   no force
no strain

8   natural action without deeds is the equilibrium of
     mankind

COMMENTARY

*Chapter Three begins to lay the foundation of learning
and education from a Taoist perspective. It emphasizes
the need for personal experience and directly making
contact with the root of all knowledge and wisdom, no
matter what the subject. In archaic Taoist language,
when referring to people or a populace, the Taoist is
always seeing the totality of himself as a community. The
different parts of his bodymind, the different spirits of his
internal organs, as well as the different parts of his mind
and intellect form a personal community of one.*

1 **MIND:** "Wise and sophisticated" refers to sacred texts and to sages with a particular philosophical bent or specific message. The "two liquids" are your own intuitive wisdom and other wisdom that comes from outside you, meaning text or other people. The "one" in this case is you.

2 **MIND:** All wisdom and advice that comes from outside of you. In this case, wisdom and advice is seen as treasure or great wealth. Can great wealth really belong to us or are we just the temporary stewards of it?

3 **HEART:** "Authentic learning" refers to intuitive/natural learning or wisdom that comes via the intuition from the Tao.

4 **BODY:** "Sound leader" is a leader who follows the Tao. "Populace" in this case can mean a community, but it can also mean the different parts of your personality.

5 **MIND:** An "open heart" refers to a clear and vitalized spirit, or *shen*.

6 **MIND:** The "people" referred to are Taoist Cultivators.

7 **HAND:** These are specific instructions on how to behave inwardly and outwardly to align yourself and your actions with the Tao.

8 **HAND:** "Natural action" is a spontaneous, authentic response. "Deeds" in this case is an externally driven response, which could be physical, emotional, or intellectual.

CHAPTER FOUR

The way

1   the *tao* source of life is an empty vessel
    vast within
    vast without
    possessed of transcendental space

2   it seems able to hold anything and everything

3   yet it is also a force

4   file down the sharpest edge with it

5   untie any knot and unknot any tangle

    "problems/worries.

6   soften the harshest glare and settle unwanted dust

7   it is easy to secret away until needed
    because it is already hidden away

8   but even in subtle storage
    it seems to have a life all its own

9   nativity unknown
    it was here before the parents of humanity
    traversed the sky

    Eternal/Always been.

COMMENTARY

1-2 MIND and HAND: This is how you should view or hold the Tao in your mind. These are also specific instructions for Taoist meditation. The Cultivator sits or stands in a specific meditative pose and sees the totality of himself as a completely empty vessel that is both vast within and vast without, stretching outward in all directions to encompass the entire universe.

3 MIND: This force is one of change and balancing.

4 MIND and BODY: The "sharpest edge" refers to the abruptness of life that you encounter.

5 MIND and BODY: "Knots and tangles" refer to problems and worries.

6 MIND and BODY: "Harshest glare" represents things that you see that disturb your *shen*, or spirit. "Unwanted dust" refers to chaotic thinking.

7 MIND and HAND: "Secret away" refers to taking your cultivation—everything you do, everything you feel and meditate—and placing it to your *dantien*, which is a focal point located three-and-a-half inches below the navel and inward. Taoist Cultivators of old placed their meditation, their wisdom, everything, down into this part of their anatomy. During intermediate Taoist mediation, you feel as if you are thinking from this place. While not specifically being the navel, it is related closely to the umbilicus.

This stanza is also an injunction to regard all of your Taoist ideals, disciplines, and your cultivation of the Taoist life as a private matter; to hold it out for the whole world to see will disrupt the balance and make cultivating the *Tao* almost impossible.

8 **MIND and BODY:** A Taoist has his cultivation life, or his formal practice, which he puts away, or stores, inside himself; yet the rest of his life becomes an informal practice where his mind, his personality, and his spirit are being refined because of the regular occurrence of formal practice. Said another way, the momentum of regular formal practice continues to move through the Cultivator after the formal session. Intermediate and advanced Taoist Cultivators talk about actually feeling the Tao, the *yin* and *yang* of the Tao, turning inside the bodymind as they're going about their day-to-day activities. Once engaged, Taoist cultivation continues working even when you're not aware of it.

9 **HEART:** The Tao has existed forever. Parents of humanity refer to the inhabitants of the mythical city of

Wu, which is an ancient pre-Taoist creation myth preserved in the oral tradition. These parents of humanity, known as the emperors and empresses, flew between the heavens and the earth in sky chariots, and thus kept the two united.

CHAPTER FIVE

1   nature as creation is a relentless force

2   the relentless constantly faces the decay of its own
        fruits

3   the sound person also relentless
     faces the decay of the fruits of mankind

4   in the midst of this unsentimental force there exists
        a mysterious space
     the lungs and bellows of your universe

5   like lungs its shape changes
     like bellows its function does not occur alone

6   the more that it works
     the more that it brings forth

7   and words however eloquent
     exhaust the magic of this sacred space

8   speak not in word or labels

9   you can only feel it with your core and viscera

COMMENTARY

1 **HEART:** The creative force of nature is constantly moving, shifting, and changing.

2 **HEART:** This refers to the cyclical phases of nature: spring as birth/*yüan*, summer as growth/*heng*, fall as maturation/*li*, and winter as death/*chen*. Whatever nature creates invariably dies and is reborn.

3 **HEART:** Someone who follows the *Tao* must emulate nature and realize the life cycle of anything he says or does or creates.

4 **MIND:** At the heart of this cyclical flow, there is a transcendental space that is the entrance to the Tao Realm.

5-6 **MIND:** This entrance to the Tao Realm pulsates and changes with its own cyclical pattern. It expands (*yang*) and contracts (*yin*). Within its influence, all life is created and sustained. Taoists refer to it as the Mysterious Space.

7 HEART: Attempting to understand and describe the Mysterious Space in an intellectual manner severs your connection to it. Though language is admittedly one of mankind's most important creations, most discourse is undisciplined and drains the power of creation from the Mysterious Space.

8-9 HAND: These are instructions; embrace silence and attempt to feel the cyclical pulsations of the Mysterious Space. Listen first with your core being, called your *dantien*, a location three-and-one-half inches below your navel and inward toward the center of your bodymind. Thereafter, Taoists learn to listen to the beat of nature with their viscera, specifically the heart, lungs, liver, spleen, kidneys, and the triple warmer, which is an organ that exists in Traditional Chinese Medical theory.

CHAPTER SIX

1   the mysterious space is as silent and real as an
          imaginary
   conversation

2   and yet

3   like a fertile valley
   where two slopes meet
   in conversation

4   the root of life takes hold to yield everything
          between
   heaven and earth

5   enduring succession of continuous
   interchanging

6   the mysterious space is always there
   waiting for a director to use
   its inexhaustible gossamer strength

COMMENTARY

1 **HEART and MIND:** The Mysterious Space is the entry point to the Tao. It is experienced in reality as having the same quality as a conversation recalled in your imagination.

2–3 **HEART and MIND:** An external example from nature to describe the Mysterious Space.

4 **HEART and MIND:** Mankind is a vital part of the "everything" that exists between Heaven and Earth.

5 **HEART:** The Mysterious Space remains constant through the flux and flow of life.

6 **HAND:** The Taoist must enter the Tao through the Mysterious Space and channel and direct the force of creation he finds there. The Taoist Cultivator experiences this as if he is in the center of an ethereal web that connects him to literally everyone and everything in the universe.

CHAPTER SEVEN

1 look up
   look down
   look around

2 it has always been here

3 look up
   look down
   look around

4 it will always be here

5 infinite duration outlasting ordinary space and time

6 the universe that you perceive has always been
        here
   and will be here after you are no longer present
   to perceive it

7 because it gave birth to you and not the contrary
        to which you cling

8 rather than being one step ahead
   and asleep toward up and coming possibilities

9 the sound traveler stays two steps back
and remains awake to all that is possible

10 if you look upon yourself as an accident in space
and time

11 then you will always be present in space and time

12 it is as simple as finding yourself by not looking

13 this is a thought form for thinking into

COMMENTARY

1-4 **HAND:** These are specific meditation instructions. The Taoist meditator will look up and down thirty-six times and then trace clockwise and counterclockwise circles with his gaze in preparation for cultivating a mystic state. These eye movements sensitize the Cultivator to what he normally is unaware of in his field of vision. The circular movements of his eyes collect and condense life-force, or *qi*, to the upper *dantien*, or mind's eye. This is experienced as a gathering of radiant light energy in an area between his eyebrows and about one inch inward within his skull. This is called "Gathering the Light."

5 **HEART and HAND:** Gathering the Light induces a mystic state in which time seems to stand still or dilates to encompass everything that the Cultivator experiences.

6 **HEART:** An expression of the vastness and timelessness of the universe.

7 **HEART:** A reminder that the wonders of the universe gave birth to you.

8 **MIND:** Projected expectations and thinking ahead in speculation blinds you to the myriad possibilities contained in the universe.

9 **MIND:** A "sound traveler" is a Taoist Cultivator who turns inward and pulls back from projected expectation. Instead, the Cultivator attempts to sit and watch the Tao as it naturally unfolds within and without.

10–13 **MIND:** Most people go through life feeling that they were either created for some grand purpose or that they exist at the whim of a capricious and often cold universe. The Taoist

Cultivator, however, sees himself as a happy accident whose experience ultimately benefits everyone and everything in the universe.

)(

CHAPTER EIGHT

1   if a person wants to be at their best
    then they should pattern themselves after water

2   water serves the land and the life on the land

3   it gives this life by moving through the land
    seeking its own balance and equilibrium

4   this is in contrast to human beings who always
       look up
    and think of rising to some lofty achievement

5   water will always flow around obstacles
    and seek out the lowest earthbound opened space
       that it can find

6   in this way
    it is always closer to the miracle than we are

7   the miracle talks to us through water

8   and it says

9 wherever you choose to live remember
the earth beneath your feet
consider how to feel it with all that you do

10 whenever you want peace remember
to flow into your heartmind
plunging into the profound love that resides deep
within you

11 however difficult remember
that you should speak frankly
but never drown others with your words

12 whichever instances call for leadership remember
that a constant stream helps order
the lifeforms around it

13 whatever business you transact remember
to go steadily to the source
and dutifully perform without washing up on
unprepared land

14 if you listen to me
when there is a call to action
the miracle will tell you when it is time to act

15 contending causes contention

16 have no part of it
and you will be a cool stream
nourishing to all

COMMENTARY

1-2 BODY and HAND: Water is a metaphor that informs every facet of Taoist life and activity. Taoist art, dance, and exercise all employ the image of naturally flowing water as a model for achieving peak experience of life and living. This includes even the arts of negotiation and commerce.

3 BODY and HAND: The Taoist seeks a state of balance and equilibrium in all things as a means of connecting with the Tao Source of Life. This includes, but is not limited to, a balance between work and play, industry and leisure, sleep and wakefulness, and intellectualism and emotionalism. A balance of food types, colors, and emotions also contribute to a life informed by the Tao.

4 BODY and MIND: Excessive mental activity, a preoccupation with the inequities of life, dwelling on what could be over what is, all can cause turbid *qi*, or life-energy, to rise upward to the head, disrupting the inner workings of the bodymind.

5 MIND: Turbid *qi* infects the bodymind and creates the illusion of impediments to a happy and fulfilled life. To counter this, Taoist Cultivators will enter a reality structure in which they see themselves as a mass of water flowing around obstacles and seeking the earth. The Taoist movement art of *T'ai Chi Ch'uan* takes this notion as a founding principle.

6 HEART: Water is a perennial model of the Tao.

7–8 HEART: The idea that the spirit of the natural world speaks to human beings is a fundamental Taoist precept. Cultivators listen to the wind, rain, rivers, and lakes as a way to vibrate harmoniously with the Tao.

9 HAND: These are instructions in deliberate mindful stepping reinforced by an increased awareness of our terrestrial connection.

10 HAND: The heartmind is accessed through an energy cultivation point located beneath the breastbone. This energy locus governs feelings of peacefulness, compassion, and love. It also stabilizes the body's human spirit, or *shen*.

11–13 BODY: Speak frankly and honestly. Be a man of few words who is consistent and honorable. "Go steadily to the source" means reinforcing one's connection with the Tao.

14 **MIND:** During the direct transmission of the *Tao Te Ching*, the student is reminded that Lao-tzu himself is constantly sending a time-binding signal of wisdom that will guide and instruct the student throughout his life.

15–16 **HEART:** "Contending" equates with stubbornness, aggressiveness, overt assertiveness, and generally trying too hard.

CHAPTER NINE

1   pull an archer's bow past the limits of its
        construction
    fill a gallon jug with two gallons of water
    hone a knife to an excessively sharp edge
    stretch overly a muscle toward achievement

2   all that you get is a
    strained
    dulled split
    and broken
    deformation of the miraculous

3   if you judge yourself by material things
    that are temporarily in your possession
    you will always be worried about who will take
        possession
    of them next

4   if you are too proud of these material things
    then you are courting personal disaster

5   the *tao* source of life has some advice for you

6   pause activity
     enjoin with it
     engage poise and relaxation

COMMENTARY

1 **HEART:** These are examples of trying too hard and contending.

2 **HEART:** These are the results of contentious behavior.

3 **BODY:** This stanza warns against materialism and the mental states that can come from it. It is interesting to note that Taoists historically have been at least as concerned with spiritual materialism as they were about other forms of materialism.

4 **BODY:** Excessive pride leads to all kinds of problems that negatively affect the Cultivator and his quest for remaining connected to the Tao Source of Life.

5–6 HAND: These are instructions for connecting to the Tao Realm and Tao Source of Life.

- Assume a balanced standing or seated posture that is suitable for meditation.

- Be as still and unmoving as possible. Accomplish this not by contracting inward, but rather by seeing yourself expanding outwardly in all directions. See yourself filling up the universe.

- Endeavor to be as physically relaxed and mentally aware as possible. See yourself as a perfectly tuned violin string, poised to receive the first bow stroke of a master musician. Playfully disregard any distractions that may arise and cultivate this state of relaxed awareness for as long as you are comfortable. Taoists call this cultivating *sung*.

CHAPTER TEN

1   creative spirit
    vital soul
    wondrous bodymind

2   can you combine these into one phase
    and gently hold onto it

3   one phase one part one moment

4   can you commune with
    and direct the elemental force of life
    and enter into the rebirth of gentleness
    and be like a newborn

5   can you wash and cleanse your mystic inner vision
    while clearing it of the refuse left behind by
        ordinary sight

6   is it possible for you to stay out of your own way
    while being your own leader

7   can you stomp the earth
look to the heavens while being receptive
passive
possessed of quietude

8   can you be knowledgeable and clever
and regard it as whimsical

9   create and nourish
let all creation be the worlds
not your own

10 have fun when you work
work when you have fun

11 be a leader without appearing to be
and you will personify fine uncarved wood
in the hands of a master carpenter

12 can you guess who this master is

you (WWJD) Jesus.

COMMENTARY

1 **MIND:** These are facets of the Three Treasures: *ching* (essence), *shen* (spirit, soul) and *qi* (life-force energy).

66

Creative spirit is the drive to live an industrious and creative life.

Vital soul is the essence and power expressed by your soul.

Wondrous bodymind is your corporeal self and all its inner workings.

2–3 **HAND:** Joining the above three and being mindfully under their combined influence with all that you do lays the foundation of a Cultivator's life.

4 **HAND:** Absorbing life-force energy into your bodymind to induce a profound state of relaxation. A Taoist Cultivator engineers this by turning inward and suggesting that each part of his bodymind should release tension and fill up with blood and life-force energy. The order of this progressive relaxation is very specific: hands and fingers, arms and shoulders, back of neck and head, face and full neck, upper torso and back, mid-torso and back, lower torso and back, thighs, knees, lower legs, and finally, feet and toes. This process of progressive relaxation can take anywhere from five minutes to one hour.

5 **HAND:** After progressively relaxing from hands to feet, the Cultivator inhales and imagines drawing energy upward from the ground, filling the entire bodymind. The energy leaves the body and returns to the earth with each exhalation, taking any vestiges of tension or dis-ease [*sic*] with it. This cleansing is

inclusive and washes away mental confusions as well as physical ones.

6 HAND: Once the bodymind is conceived as being cleansed, the Cultivator imagines that his bodymind is a conduit of outflowing *qi* coming to him from the Tao Realm via the Mysterious Space. The Cultivator holds the notion that he is not controlling the life-force, instead he makes himself a fit receptacle for it.

7 HAND: These are instructions:

"Stomp …": Lightly stomping the feet stabilizes the mystic state.

"Look … heavens …": Look inward while maintaining a light, buoyant, and sensitive energy at the crown of the head.

" … of quietude": The quiescent state induced by this meditation is called *rur-jing*.

8 MIND: The Cultivator's overall mental state.

9 BODY: Under the influence of this technique, the Taoist is inspired to paint, write, play, or engage in creation of some kind. The Taoist creates for the good of all by projecting the nourishing energy of creation to his environs and beyond.

10 MIND and BODY: In all areas of your life, perform with active engagement and intense interest tempered by whimsy and happiness.

11 HEART: Open up to the Tao Source and allow it to move you; to influence, initiate, and support your actions.

12 MIND: The Master in this case is the *Tao* expressing itself through your bodymind. To the Taoist, this is the ultimate act of nourishment for both the Cultivator and his community.

CHAPTER ELEVEN

1   here is a lesson for you

2   imagine thirty separate pieces of stick all cut to a
        uniform length

3   visualize the single sticks
     and look at the two ends that are a part of each
        and every one of
     them

4   end middle end

5   these thirty wooden sticks all have the power to
        unite to form the
     hub of a
     great wheel

6   in the process of this uniting
     they give birth to the center of the hub

7   by sacrificing their individuality they magically
        create
     the utility of the wheel

8 take a lump of clay and expand the enclosed
   center within
and a vessel is created

9 it is this expanded enclosure that makes the vessel
   useful

10 likewise a structure does not make a space and
   shape for living
space and shape are necessary for living

11 all of this is called creation through not-being

12 not-being creates the intangible

13 the intangible creates utility of the tangible

COMMENTARY

1-7 MIND: In archaic Taoist language, imagery of thirty units relates to the intuitive mind. The *Tao* speaks to us through our intuition. These flashes of awareness come to us from quarters that are generally silent. The first step to awakening your intuitive mind is to see yourself as an integrated and purposeful whole rather than as a collection of parts. Furthermore, the invocation of the self as the center of a circle (the hub of a great wheel) is to see yourself as part of a transcendental shape that contains the totality of existence. You assume this transcendental nature yourself. Simply put, pretending that you are the hub of a ceaselessly turning universe triggers the intuition and invites it to speak and act spontaneously. The Chinese call this spontaneity *tzu-jan*.

8–9 **MIND:** Metaphorically, each of us is a "lump of clay." All we have to do is expand and shape the centers of ourselves to allow wisdom to flow into us via our intuition.

10 **MIND and HEART:** A life truly lived is an authentic one that occurs spontaneously without being contrived, planned, or restricted.

11–13 **HAND and HEART:** Creating through not-being is allowing the soul to take the lead of our lives. It speaks to us in a language of sensation, emotion, and imagery that comes to us through our intuition. We have but to listen to it and respond accordingly.

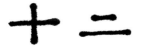

CHAPTER TWELVE

1   imagine a soft light of blue-green
    imagine a strong red light
    imagine a rich yellow light
    imagine a bright white light
    now imagine the black absence of color

2   if you look at these lights singly you will know
        what they are

3   if you allow them into your eyes all at once
    then you will not be able to distinguish one from
        the other

4   the twelve musical notes can be arranged
        magically to create a
    joyful noise

5   the twelve musical notes can also be thrown
        together without
    method
    like stones in a hole
    that becomes an ordinary activity that denies
        the hole its usefulness

6   attempt to
    eat something sour
    eat something bitter
    eat something sweet
    eat something pungent
    eat something salty
    all at the same time and the once pleasant tastes
        are likely to
    nauseate you

7   ordinary people exceed the basic goodness of the
        things of this
    world
    in searching for new ways to exceed themselves

8   the momentum of exceeding unbalances the
        heartmind
    and generates insecurity and a loose footing that
        denies the true self

9   for these reasons
    the sound person speaks to the unconscious heartmind
    requesting instructions on how to nourish the true self

10 when gently asked
    the unconscious teaches appreciation for those
        things that are
    within us

11 all

12 when gently asked
   the unconscious teaches circumspection for those
        things that are
   without us

13 all

COMMENTARY

1 **HAND and MIND:** Taoists employ visualization as a primary tool for cultivation. Much of this visualization involves a self-directed investigation into the inner workings of the bodymind. Cultivators discovered that fixing the imagination on specific colors balances the life-force energy, or *qi*, of the various internal body organs. This led to the Five Element Theory of correspondences that has been applied to all phases of Chinese art, science, and culture.

2 **HAND and MIND:** The idea of experiencing life—even one's own—as a balance of five specific energies involves cultivating an intimate relationship with each.

3 MIND: An intimate relationship with the different energies/*qi* of the bodymind is impossible without the ability to isolate one kind of energy from another.

4 MIND: Music is a powerful force. The twelve notes relate directly to the twelve different kinds of *qi* that blend together to form the *qi* of the Universal. The *qi* of the Universal, in turn, forms all matter and energy in the universe. While most Taoist music is pentatonic (five notes) in nature, Cultivators employ twelve different notes as objects of Taoist meditation.

5 MIND and BODY: Cultivating an authentic life requires a specific method. Spontaneity/*tzu-jan* can occur only within a limiting structure. Limits yield intensity. The image of music created "without method" becomes a Taoist metaphor for a misspent life; to wit, a life created without method reduces it to something as common as rocks and stone.

6 HAND and MIND: Attempting to experience life indiscriminately, without method, all at once, and without patience can make one spiritually sick.

7 BODY: Exceeding in this case invokes a state of inevitable dissatisfaction brought on by attempting to do too much too soon.

8 HEART: The dissonant energy created by exceeding interferes with your connection to the Tao Source of

Life. This leads to feelings of dread and insecurity that, if left unchecked, eventually result in a rejection of the Tao Way of Life altogether.

9–13 **HEART:** Listening to the soul and the wisdom it imparts is vital to the Taoist. The "heartmind," or *yi*, is the way to speak to the soul and ultimately to the Tao itself. This method of speaking is expressed practically as a wave of loving compassion and understanding extended to the deepest parts of one's own self.

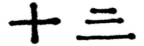

CHAPTER THIRTEEN

1 life and death
favor and disgrace
praise and blame
success and failure

2 all of these conditions confuse and dismay us
because
they are the same ailment
they cause ill at ease states and related worries

3 how does this happen

4 when favor is acquired so is the fear of losing
favor acquired

5 if someone thinks that the corporeal body is the
limit of the self
then the fear that is inherent in the body makes
itself known
and is difficult to subdue

6 how can you trust and accept your corporeal limits
in the face of
fear

7   we have fear when a limited self is absorbed in
        importance

8   if you view the unlimited world as the self
        then you can be trusted with it

9   because only the person who sees the world as
        themselves
        and their self as the world

10 will take care of it

COMMENTARY

1-2 **MIND:** This is a restatement of the lessons in
Chapter Two. The discriminating mind will, through
the act of creating opposite extremes, confuse and
damage us.

3-4 **MIND:** The act of creating extremes ultimately
engenders a deep-seated fear.

5 **HEART:** Seeing yourself as a limited being naturally
leads to an unreasonable fear of the world around you.

6–7 **MIND:** Fear is generated when we become self-absorbed and self-indulgent. An exaggerated sense of one's own importance renders you untrustworthy. It also prevents you from accepting the totality of both your personal gifts and deficits.

8–10 **HEART:** This is a statement of Taoist identification. These stanzas explain how a Taoist must view himself. They also present the idea of Taoist stewardship of the world.

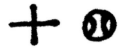

CHAPTER FOURTEEN

1 talking about the character of the *tao* source of life
      is fundamentally
   useless
   talking about the lessons of the *tao* way of life is
      likewise useless

2 because the real way is a revealed way

3 awakened in yourself
   only through an imitation
   of the way
   as yourself

4 but where are the clues to this awakening

5 look all around yourself deliberately
   and attempt to see the nothing that is
   deliberately all around yourself

6 nothing no thing nothing

7 if you cannot see it
   then you are in its presence

8 try to listen deliberately
to the space between the sounds
of your deliberate world

9 if you do not hear anything
then you will be hearing it through its absence

10 grab hold of something with your hand and let it go
now imagine some things that you cannot grab
      with either your
hand or mind
then you will surely be holding it

11 invisible inaudible intangible

12 the form and function of these three components
      blend together
creating the *tao* way of life

13 do not think of it as upper and lower or dark and
      bright or rise and
sink
instead view the miracle as something that is
      continuously moving
unnamable and totally elusive

14 it is a formless form and a methodless method
that gives birth to an image of no thing

15 when you confront it
there is no face to look at

16 when you pursue it
   there is no shape to follow

17 it does not *tao* talk
   it does not *tao* act

18 but if you look for the wisdom that it leaves in its
        wake
   and deal with present realities accordingly

19 then you will have seized the beginning moment
   that is the *tao* way of living

COMMENTARY

1 **MIND and HEART:** Discourse about and
intellectual investigation into the nature of the *Tao* is a
dead end.

2 **HEART:** The authentic Taoist Source and Way of
Life can only be grasped and understood intuitively. It
is beyond intellectual understanding. The authentic
way is mystically revealed to the Cultivator.

3 BODY and HEART: Awaken to the Tao within you by awakening your intuition. Engineer this awakening by imitating the Tao in your day-to-day life.

4–10 HAND: These are meditative instructions that generate an awakening to the Tao Source of Life and support of the Tao Way of Life.

11–12 MIND: When the Cultivator begins to be subtly aware of the invisible, inaudible, and intangible aspects of the Tao Way of Life, a sense of the totality of the Tao begins to manifest in his consciousness.

13 MIND: Another way of saying this is that the Tao cannot be experienced when viewing extremes. Rather, it is readable between the lines or hearable between the beats of your heart.

14 HAND: All Taoist methods of cultivation are judged according to this standard.

15–16 MIND: These stanzas establish the idea of the practicing Taoist as a "hunter of the way."

17 HEART: An alternate translation of this stanza could be:

> it does not sound the way you would expect it to sound
>
> it does not act in the way you would expect it to act.

18–19 BODY: You know the Tao Way of Living by the signs it leaves behind. This is akin to a hunter tracking an animal through the wilderness. By examining the animal's tracks, its leavings, as well as broken twigs and other signs, the hunter comes to intrinsically know the size, shape, and character of the creature. He is able to discern the animal's direction of travel. Eventually, though unseen by one another, the beast and the hunter begin to share a common bond. In Taoist terms, this bond is "seizing the beginning moment."

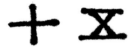

CHAPTER FIFTEEN

1 sage wise men of ancient space and time
were agents of the *tao* source of life
and as such appeared mysterious and intent
as they perceived the sacred voices and the subtle
    clues
of the miracle and its injunctions

2 their trance of wisdom was so profound
that they seem distant and removed
yet present and intrigued
as they gave their full attention
to observe the smallest of happenings
and while this behavior was beyond ordinary
    understanding
it can be described without looking to the mind

3 calculating yet spontaneous
a revealed attentiveness of a hunter crossing a
    frozen stream

4 fearless yet tentative
they behaved as if the teacher's teacher had
    placed a knife at every
quarter to keep them alert and aware

5 dignified yet playful
they conducted themselves as if to be the courteous guest of
everyone that they met

6 humble yet resolute
they deferred to the ordinary forces around them without
submission and looked like ice yielding in the sun

7 authentic and unspoiled
they acted with honest simplicity as if the depth of their beings
were composed of concentrated innocence

8 receptive and approachable
they presented a rarefied space of sanctuary and repose inviting to
all

9 carefree and gently demanding
they blended freely with nature and with people but did not
sacrifice their own inner direction

10 the ancient child asks
who is it that can find quiet among the noise

11 the sage wise man sits comfortably still
and can lay down amidst the confusion

12 the ancient child asks
who is it that can remain calm and seize the
moment

13 through engaged activity the sage wise man
preserves his life and
the life around him

14 to embrace the *tao* way of life is to seek emptiness
as a means to avoiding spiritual materialism
and the entropy it induces

15 by not seeking accomplishment
you become endless and vitalized
continually

COMMENTARY

This chapter tells you how to live your life to emulate the Tao.

1 **MIND and BODY:** This paints a picture of people who live a mystic lifestyle.

2 **MIND and BODY:** The last two lines reiterate something said previously; to wit, from a Taoist

perspective, you can't understand the sage's behavior with a rational mind. It is beyond ordinary reasoning, thinking, and logic.

3–9 **MIND and BODY:** This stanza begins listing examples of the way a Taoist should live his life. The first line of these seven stanzas presents a pair of opposites that must be balanced one against the other. In the midst of balancing the two concepts, the Taoist behavior appears.

4 **MIND and BODY:** "The teacher's teacher" is a reference to the forces of nature, to Mother Nature, in western literature. Behaving as if a knife is placed at every quarter refers to a Taoist meditative technique in which the Cultivator remains completely still and is uniformly attentive to every aspect of his bodymind in all directions.

10–11 **HAND:** These stanzas are a question and a response. The initiator, speaking for Lao-tzu, asks the question in stanza 10. The student answers accordingly in stanza 11. These are specific meditative instructions.

12–13 **HAND:** The Master questions and the student responds. In stanza 13, "engaged activity" is, from a Taoist perspective, activity that is mindful, spontaneous, and playful.

14–15 MIND and BODY: "Spiritual materialism," which the Taoist continually avoids, refers to emotional or intellectual baggage that ultimately gets in the way, separating the Cultivator from the Tao Source.

Justinus / Justus

Hailey   Justin

                    Justice

different spellings

Heylee / Hailee
          Hailie

Haleigh / Haley /

Hayleigh / Hayley / Haylie

90

Ceaseless / faithful /

our love is ✝ 𝄞 *ceaseless*

CHAPTER SIXTEEN

1   deliver all your inner confusion to the earth
    and resting quietly
    leave your mind undisturbed

2   allow all things that manifest and their roots
    to assume definite shape
    and move about in activity
    against the backdrop of your reflective awareness
    and observe these events passively with a
        controlled heart and
    simple spirit

3   when these bustling shapes slow down and cease
        in their activity
    and return to the nothingness from whence they
        came
    you will attain a state of quietude
    that is an imitation of the *tao* way of life
    without force it occurs naturally
    and is called ceaseless and faithful
    it is known as the law of mundane transposition
    in this state you will see yourself as you truly are
    this perspective must shock you a little
    or it will not be genuine as a picture of your true self

91

4   understanding this law of mundane transposition
    begets tolerance of self and others

5   understanding tolerance of self and others
    begets wisdom of self and others

6   understanding the wisdom of self and others
    begets infinite insight into self and others

7   employing the insight of self and others creates
        resonance with
    the heavens
    the earth
    and man

8   employing this resonance
    creates an alignment with the *tao* way of life

9   thus aligned you will directly communicate with the
        miracle
    and even in ordinary death will forever be a part of it

COMMENTARY

Chapter Sixteen consists entirely of meditative instructions.

1 HAND and MIND: "Inner confusion," refers to pain, guilt, emotion, worries, troubles, and so forth. "Allowing things [to] manifest and their roots" refers to the subsequent thoughts triggered by the original confusions. The Cultivator must allow all these thoughts to quiet down.

2 HAND and MIND: "Reflective awareness" in Taoist meditation is explained in the following line, which tells the Cultivator to view his mental contents with a passive, detached manner.

3 HAND and MIND: This stanza discusses what happens when the Cultivator views the workings of his consciousness with a passive and detached manner. Meditating in this way allows the Cultivator to imitate the Tao Way of Life. In this case, the facet of the Tao Way of Life that is being imitated is its energetic quality. When the meditator passively observes the inner workings of his own bodymind, his consciousness clears and his *qi* energy begins to smooth out and resemble the *qi* energy of nature that is all around him. Nature's *qi* represents the energy of the Tao.

4 MIND: Simply put, the "law of mundane transposition" is allowing the dissociated *qi* energy that is generated by everyday ordinary thinking to transpose into a smooth *qi* energy that vibrates harmoniously with the Tao Source of Life.

5–8 MIND: These stanzas tell the Taoist what occurs with ever-increasing levels of skill at performing mundane transposition.

9 MIND and HEART: The miracle is the Tao itself. The Cultivator remains a part of it even when he appears to die. Taoists believe in the literal impossibility of death, because everything is part of the Tao Source.

CHAPTER SEVENTEEN

1 this is a warning

2 beware the constraints of looking
and ceasing to see

3 the seeds of chaos that were sown

4 by the sons and daughters
of the emperors and empresses

5 are buried in the soil
where they can do no harm to your essential
    nature

6 you must protect the ancestral treasures
your lifeforce
your essence
your spirit

7 benevolent altruism
honest authority
observed ceremony
the songs of creativity

8   cannot be managed
by any manner of collective intent

9   to govern through the *tao* way of life
is to do so without notice
and remain invisible to the world

10 to govern by the *tao* way of life
granting light and sound to the eyes and ears
attracts the heartmind and heart spirit of the world

11 to govern through light and sound
without the *tao* way of life
engenders the fear of the world

12 to govern by unwise force
alone
breeds hatred in the world that nourish the seeds
   of chaos

13 having faith in the faithless
destroys the heart of man
and they become sleeping automatons driven by
   words and labels
and words as drugs

14 the method of the true self as original nature
is all that is needed
to embody
to accomplish
wonders

COMMENTARY

1-2 MIND and HEART: "Looking and ceasing to see" describes a mind that is hypnotized by illusion.

3-5 MIND: These stanzas refer to an ancient Chinese creation myth in which the populace was thrown into chaos because it stopped looking at things as they truly were and started to see all sorts of fanciful illusions.

"Buried in the soil" refers to dissolution.

"Looking and ceasing to see," or being hypnotized by an illusion, is endemic in human culture and is a function of our neurology interacting with our universe. But there's no karmic momentum to looking and ceasing to see. Lao-tzu is saying that the sins of the father will not be visited on the son.

6 HAND: Your life-force is called *qi*. Your essence is *ching*. Your spirit is *shen*. These are the three vital forces that combine to make you a living, breathing human being.

7-8 BODY: The life of a human being cannot be run by committee. These stanzas are an affirmation of

Taoist individualism. "Benevolent altruism" refers to doing good works for the good of the world and the community. "Honest authority" is being resolute and forthright. "Observed ceremony" is ritual. "Songs of creativity" is an archaic reference to all sorts of creative acts. Stanza 8 says that a king, a ruler, a government, or even a religion cannot govern these acts among people. An individual must govern himself.

9–12 BODY and HAND: "To govern" in archaic Taoist language has virtually nothing to do with governing a group of people, a community, a city, or a kingdom. To govern in this case is to govern oneself; to govern one's intellect, one's passions, one's energy, and one's life.

Stanza 9 outlines the best way to govern oneself.

Stanza 10 outlines the second best way to govern yourself.

Stanza 11 outlines a less-than-desirable way to govern oneself.

Stanza 12 outlines the worst way to govern oneself.

13 MIND and BODY: If you have "faith in the faithless," from a Taoist perspective, you become hypnotized into a waking sleep where you are governed by illusions ("words as labels" and "words as drugs").

14 HEART: "The method of the true self as original nature" is the Taoist definition for cultivation.

+)(CHAPTER EIGHTEEN

1   for the decline of the *tao* way of life
begins with prisons of the bodymind
and externally applied rules of the bodymind

2   defined allegiance
justice blind
equity bound in invisible knots

3   when judicious thought is the goal
and not thinking
intelligence leads to observed contrast
supplanting the thinking moment

4   faithless ceremonies are created
that disturb the bodymind

5   the bodymind is a family
harmonious when

6   open absence
blends with
full presence

7 serene when

8 full presence
blends effortlessly with
will, thought, and imagination

9 a natural coalescence

10 will, thought, and imagination
meet and support
the lifeforce

11 this simple assemblage
speaking directly to the heart spirit
results in a myriad of actions
filled with spontaneity and naturalness

12 composed and at rest
this family
playing in a field of spontaneous interaction
enjoys peaceful congress with
the shape and void

13 when the bodymind
is forced
and ill at ease

14 insincere devotion
to the bodymind
manifests itself
and spills over to every facet of life

15 rejection of the *tao* way of life
can be checked only through compassion
for the self
for others

16 then reclamation of the original nature of mankind
can begin

17 the ancient child asks me to enumerate the steps

18 the open absence of the bodymind
must combine and share with
the closed presence of the bodymind

19 the closed presence of the bodymind
must combine and share with
the mind intent of the bodymind

20 the mind intent of the bodymind
must combine and share with
the lifeforce of the bodymind

21 the lifeforce of the bodymind
must combine and share with
the heart spirit of the bodymind

22 the heart spirit of the bodymind
must combine and share with
the spontaneous actions of the bodymind

23 the spontaneous actions of the bodymind
   must combine and share with
   the shape and the void

COMMENTARY

1 **MIND:** This refers to restrictions of thought and behavior imposed by an outside source or authority.

2 **MIND:** "Equity bound in invisible knots" is the Taoist phrase for a low standard of achievement.

3 **MIND:** Thought, or thinking, in this case is a fossilized concept that is no longer growing, or something that people decide to accept as fact without feeling the necessity to constantly rethink it so that opinions and observations may change over time as more information becomes available.

4 **MIND:** This stanza particularly attacks Confucian ritual that the Taoists regarded, by and large, as mindlessly observed social obligations.

5 **BODY and HAND:** Taoists believed that a man who "looks and ceases to see" will come to regard

his bodymind as a collection of chaotic individual parts that argue, fight, and break down. The idea that the parts go together to make a family that naturally seeks to live in harmony forms the basis of many Taoist cultivation activities.

6 BODY and HAND: "Open absence" refers to the "empty spoon," which is the Taoist image for an open mind that is uncluttered by fossilized beliefs and opinions. You must be open before you can be filled with your own presence—not someone else's but your own.

7 BODY and HAND: Being filled with your own essence leads to a state of serenity or calmness.

8 BODY and HAND: Living in a state of calm serenity eventually leads to being fully present in the moment. The Cultivator brings that full presence to the actions of your will, thought, and imagination.

9 BODY and HAND: This full blending of will, thought, and imagination is the personification of the Taoist natural order.

10 BODY and HAND: Will, thought, and imagination that is blended effortlessly with the Cultivator's bodymind resting in the full presence of the moment, draws large amounts of life-force energy, or *qi*, from the universe all around.

11 BODY and HAND: This bodymind now fully present and under the influence of an ever-increasing life-force energy begins to open up the heart spirit. With the heart spirit open, any natural activity will yield authentic movement, life, and behavior. This is an outline of how a Taoist Cultivator should live his life.

12 MIND and HAND: Shape refers to the universe itself that you can experience, and the void is the Realm of the Tao Source of Life.

13–14 MIND and HAND: Stanza 13 warns against forcing the process. This process must be allowed to evolve naturally. Both stanzas together are specific criticisms on the way Confucians live their lives, allowing "insincere devotion" to "spill over into every facet of life."

15–16 MIND and HAND: When insincere devotion does affect the Cultivator's life, it causes an automatic severing of the connection between the Cultivator and the Tao Source of Life. This severing is called the rejection of the Tao Way of Life in archaic Taoist thinking.

Being gentle with yourself when this connection is severed is the surest way to reestablish it.

17 MIND and HEART: Lao-tzu speaking through the initiator asks the student to enumerate the steps a

Cultivator must take to reclaim his original nature. This reclamation is a mystic endeavor and lifelong Taoist pursuit.

18–23 HAND: These stanzas are known as the Six Combinations—one stanza per combination. The Cultivator must engineer these six combinations to accomplish Taoist mystical transformation. The last line refers to identifying all of your spontaneous actions as being actions of the Tao Source moving through your bodymind.

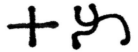

CHAPTER NINETEEN

1   absolve yourself of the need or desire to be wise
        and sophisticated
    cast off reliance on the frozen thought forms and
        constructs
    that support domesticated behavior
    and all life that you meet will benefit exponentially

2   give up
    sham beneficence
    false order
    civilized equity
    and enjoy the true fallibility of the bodymind

3   then the inner family and its outward reflection

4   will be serene and commune
    harmoniously

5   reject the practice of manipulating the flow of
        living

6   realize that life will wither
    in the harsh light of utility
    as it becomes an external thing

7   to be despoiled
    compromised

8   the miracle can only be grasped
    through gentle permission given

9   to oneself

10 but this alone will not complete the approach

11 innocent and simple steps must be taken
    to reclaim your original nature
    these steps must be artless and unadorned

12 turn inward
    search the bodymind
    for the unspoiled canvas
    upon which your life is painted

13 with open hands and arms
    absorb the powerful simplicity
    of your own self
    in its lost and genuine embrace

14 restrain the prejudiced
    and narcissistic self
    turning outward
    to glimpse within

15 regulate unrestrained need and desire
by extending the plain self
into the moments
created by looking and not seeing

16 indulging in insecure thoughts and worry for their
own sake
exhausts your connection to life's energy and flow

COMMENTARY

1 MIND and BODY: These are specific instructions about how the Taoist must think and behave. "Domesticated behavior" is mindless living as opposed to mindful living—being hypnotized by the momentum of life and consensual experience rather than being able to see the heart of it.

2 BODY: The Cultivator must give up these inauthentic, externally imposed behaviors and points of view and simply enjoy the fact that he is imperfect.

3 MIND and BODY: The "inner family" refers to the inner workings of you and your personality.

4 MIND and BODY: Being "serene and commun[ing] harmoniously" refers to all of your internal body organs, your personality, your mind, your breath, your blood, your life-force energy all working together as they should. If you accomplish all of the instructions in stanza 2, then your inner world and your outer world will come together. This is the Taoist definition of wellness.

5 BODY: This stanza tells the Taoist to get out of the way and allow life to unfold the way it wants.

6-7 BODY: This is the Taoist definition of a creative life. Creative art need not be useful other than for its appreciation during the period of its existence.

8-9 BODY: The Tao can be secured to your life only if you invite it in, if you allow it in. You cannot force the Tao into your life.

10 MIND: The right frame of mind by itself will not allow you to grasp the Tao Source of Life.

11 HAND: These are specific instructions. Your approach to cultivating the *Tao* in your daily life must be plain and childlike.

12 HAND: This is a specific Taoist meditative technique wherein the Cultivator looks for his original self.

13 **HAND:** This is a specific *qigong* activity in which the Cultivator opens his outstretched arms to absorb the power of the Tao. The "lost and genuine embrace" refers to that which we have been separated from.

14 **MIND, BODY, and HAND:** This enjoins the Taoist to look outside himself and observe nature so he can better understand the workings of nature inside himself.

15 **MIND, BODY, and HAND:** This is a specific injunction for the Cultivator to control his emotions and to project himself deeply into every event in spacetime that comes his way.

16 **MIND, BODY, and HAND:** If you are insecure and worry needlessly, you will sever your connection to life-force energy flowing into your bodymind.

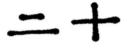

CHAPTER TWENTY

1   is there any difference
    in saying
    yes
    loudly and with force
    and saying
    yes
    softly with smiling eyes

2   between those words

3   whispers weighed
    whispered whole

4   resides the same smoothed hub of assent
    that is
    my heart

5   who are you
    I am the ancient child

6   what some say is
    good
    magnificent
    correct

7 others will say is
 bad
 decadent
 flawed

8 know that
 I refuse
 this stultifying jest

9 and say that
 each day which is
 a beginning for you
 is an end for another

10 but to me
 at least
 a thing cannot be correct

11 if indeed
 it is not flawed

12 am I to be compelled
 by false evidence
 and looming reality

13 when that which men truly fear
 is merely
 themselves seen in each other

14 the next step is natural
pervasive
take and put comfort in your soul

15 bodyminds at ease playing in the fires of sacrifice
and growth

16 singing of success and good fortune
brings nourishment to the wanderer
yourself
as new growth in the spring

17 I pretend that I am floating
solemnly and alone
engineering quietude
allowing tranquillity

18 my thoughts as grains of sand
released from the hand of my mind
to fall
alone and restful
each thought finding its own place
of stillness

19 I must form a balance between the world of man
about me
and the world of man inside of me

20 if they gather
then I am alone

21 if they are abundant
then I am desolate

22 if they are bereft
then I bring them together in joy

23 if the white thought is exhausted
then I bring them self-assurance

24 patiently I move
seeking rest for each moment in space and time
conforming to the gifts of the moment
like the water to the shoreline
helping the families
within and without
to join purposes and grasp and listen and
comprehend

25 I stand alone

26 for even in a crowd
my simple way is innocently direct and elemental
and unique
by that I am singular
rendered aimless and complete
as I absorb the earth's yellow center and lifeforce

COMMENTARY

1–2 HEART: This is a backhanded injunction for the Cultivator to give himself over to the Taoist lifestyle. In answer to the stated question, "Is there any difference?," the answer is, "No." No matter what the intent, the affirmative is the same.

3 HAND: The English words "weighed" and "whole" were chosen, in part, because their sounds reflect the mystic Taoist sounds that the Cultivator makes in order to stimulate his heart (*hway*) and his spirit (*ho*).

4 HAND: Softly aspirating those sounds from stanza 3 balance the heart and the *shen* (spirit) of the Cultivator. The heart-spirit is "the smoothed hub of assent" to the Tao.

5 HEART: It is a fundamental Taoist concept that, if you are a Taoist, you ultimately have the ability to channel the spirit and personality of Lao-tzu.

6–11 MIND and HEART: These stanzas detail the dichotomy and the interplay of *yin* and *yang*. They put forth the Taoist concept of the perfection of imperfection.

12 MIND: "False evidence" in this case is someone else's reasoning or someone else's truth. This reasoning and truth can engender only fear in the Cultivator. "Looming reality" is the result of falling under the sway of the false evidence.

13 MIND: This is a Taoist way of saying, "We have met the enemy, and he is us."

14–15 HAND: The Taoist soul is a vital part of the self and is the Cultivator's emissary to the Tao Source of Life.

16 MIND: This is a definition of fundamental Taoist optimism.

17 HAND: These are instructions in the first stage of a Taoist meditation.

18 HAND: This is the second stage of that same meditation in which the Cultivator practices non-attachment to thought.

19–22 HAND and BODY: This is the third stage of the meditation. It is also an injunction of how to behave toward others.

23 HAND and BODY: In esoteric Taoist physiology, white is the color associated with the lungs. "White thought" in this instance is excessive thinking or unbridled intellectual speculation that destroys the life-force energy of the lungs and eventually that of the kidneys.

24 HAND: "The families" in this instance are the Cultivator's inner and outer worlds. These are instructions to the Cultivator to engage in mindful activity in order to bridge those worlds.

25 HAND: This is Taoist meditation instruction: find a spot in nature and, simply, stand alone.

26 HAND: These are specific *qigong* instructions. The Taoist Cultivator standing alone actively imagines that he is absorbing the earth's life-force directly into his bodymind. The life-force is envisioned as being yellow, which is the color associated with the spleen and with "the center" in Chinese Five Element Theory.

CHAPTER TWENTY-ONE

1 courage
  integrity
  intellect
  mind
  respect

2 all these names
  and honored upright human character
  are the strengths that flow from the *tao* way of life
  emerging from a mystic pass
  invisible
  as an ever-elusive source

3 for the *tao* source of living has no shape or form
  that can be perceived in ordinary waking
        consciousness
  it is the invisible center of all shapes
  the marrow of all forms and hidden quintessence

4 the present and the past conspire
  to hide the name and secret from you

5 stomp your heels to reveal the conspiracy
  as points of fire rise in the blackness of ages past

6   the inner sense of this mystery gives you comfort
    and has always been felt by man
    but vital nourishment comes only when you chew
         on the *tao* way of
    life

7   externalized shapes beyond the apparent confines
         as manifested
    forms
    behave as a paternal fool entertaining time itself

8   by touching the earth beneath your feet
    you solidify the moment and know the name

9 of quintessence unrevealed

COMMENTARY

1 **HEART:** These are Taoist ideals.

2 **MIND:** The Cultivator being stretched evenly
between the heavens and the earth is the "mystic
pass."

3 **HEART:** This is a statement of elemental Taoist
authenticity: this is it!

4 **MIND:** Your experience of time as something that has a beginning, a middle, and an end, as something that passes. This illusion can sever your connection to the Tao Source of Life.

5 **HAND:** These are *qigong* instructions. The gentle and deliberate stomping of the feet clears the thought process.

6 **HAND:** Taoists ingest air—actually "chew it"—as a way of ingesting the *qi* of the universe. Taoists saw Cultivators as people who consumed the Tao as sustenance.

7 **MIND:** This is a Taoist injunction to avoid seeing the world as something that is outside yourself.

8–9 **HEART:** Fundamentally, Taoists must viscerally absorb the truth of their terrestrial connection no matter what their loftier ideals.

CHAPTER TWENTY-TWO

1. bend the waist   as pliable yellow gold
   flex the joints   in the shape of metal
   twist the limbs   as a tree

2. integral growth

3. make yourself an empty vessel
   and receive the lifeforce of the universal

4. see yourself as deep and vast
   yet softly muted to the ordinary world

5. standing alone under the sky
   this firmament over your accepted perceptions

6. is perpetual renewal in which the smallest piece of
   wealth

7. is a vast natural fortune
   unnoticed
   unless the heavens are above your head

8 this message is so utterly simple
that it is easily confused by over-thinking

9 when heaven is in your head
rather than above it
you will be scattered into space
without a home

10 but when heaven is in its place in the sky
real comprehension and
conscious comprehension
remain fixed to the core center in balance

11 then
you have returned home

12 an insightful person embraces and holds the absolute
singularity reflected as the original mind
consuming the consummate

13 and becomes a limitless model
of plenary usage

14 containing all the possibilities
of all that is possible

15 remain esoteric and invite wisdom
deny light to ordinary eyes
and sound to ordinary ears

16 in order to balance the mind and clear perception

17 though this ongoing quest is a personal endeavor
refrain from forcing life to be about yourself

18 do not force the hearts and spirits of others
in self-gratification
for this damages your vitality and essence

19 denial of accolades from yourself and others
to yourself
is a way to balance the conscious ordinary
comprehension
with real comprehension

20 in this way the ordinary world
will be at peace with you
and you with it

21 all of this requires you to remain adaptable
to the ever-changing present

22 bend   flex   twist
pliable gold   shaping metal   living tree

23 yes
surely these are watchwords
that preserve the integral gifts of human
existence

24 in that
   they belong to all

COMMENTARY

1 **HAND:** These are actual *qigong* instructions. When you bend the waist, you should envision yourself as "pliable yellow gold." When you flex your joints, you see yourself "in the shape of metal," which, from the Chinese perspective, is round. When you twist your limbs, you see yourself as a firmly rooted tree with limbs twisting and swaying in the breeze.

2 **HAND:** This is what results when you follow the instructions in stanza 1. "Integral growth" is wellness.

3–5 **HAND and HEART:** These are specific meditation instructions. "Accepted perceptions" are those beliefs and rationalizations that all human beings create to cope with the demands of everyday life. The Cultivator doesn't feel bad about having created these often false rationalizations; he merely accepts them as an inevitable part of the human experience.

6 HAND and HEART: "Perpetual renewal" is a fundamental Taoist concept. It plainly states that the Cultivator is in charge of the quality of his or her existence, life, and fate. The "smallest piece of wealth" in this case is a small, pure accomplishment. Think of it as a personal best, the size and shape of which changes at any given moment. There is not a rigid standard of right or wrong when engaged in cultivation. You can only be more or less essentially correct at any given time. While you are fully engaged in your play with the perfection of imperfection, it is an accomplishment to grab just a little bit of something that leans in the direction of perfection. In the land of "perpetual renewal," just that little bit will move mountains.

7 HAND and HEART: The Cultivator must specifically visualize the heavens as being something that is above him. This causes a physiological response in the Cultivator's bodymind that allows the process of perpetual renewal to actually take place.

8 MIND: Avoid looking too closely at the idea of Heaven being above your head. Regard it as an afterthought.

9–11 HAND: These are specific instructions for the Taoist Cultivator. During meditation, normal everyday activity, or any formal cultivation technique, the Cultivator is required to maintain a light, buoyant, and sensitive energy at the crown of his head. It's as if the stars themselves are about to lift him into the sky. When he does this, turbid, or confused, *qi* energy sinks and a clear *qi* rises. This allows profound intuitive thinking to take place.

12 HEART and HAND: This is a specific meditation that is designed to cultivate Taoist insight.

13-14 MIND: These are the results of cultivating Taoist insight.

15-16 HAND: This is an injunction to remain so completely still in meditation that no one can see you and no one can hear you.

17-21 BODY: These are specific instructions on the best ways to interact with other people.

22-23 HAND: "Bending," "flexing," and "twisting" are specific activities that you physically perform. "Pliable gold," "shaping metal," and a "living tree" are how you should see yourself as you move.

24 HEART: This is a Taoist concept of the ultimate empowerment of all—not just the rich, the powerful, or the educated.

CHAPTER TWENTY-THREE

1   indulged fascination of thoughts
    your own
    revealed as words of one
    disturb the fabric
    disturb the gifts
    of these singular moments
    of quintessence revealed

2   for speech is a blessing if managed
    to yourself and others

3   the same speech is a curse if not managed
    to yourself and others

4   words that intrude will damage essence and
        vitality

5   the core of both the speaker and the witness
    will be harmed when the event is filled

6   not-intruding is the natural way of optimistic *tao*
        nature
    for *tao* nature *tao* speaks not in *tao* words

7 having no-thing to say
   it can say everything

8 and does

9 expressive *tao* nature rises in a continuous stream
      that moves
   across the land
   but it must exhaust itself as part of the natural
      order
   and give support and rest to the receptive side of
      existence
   for everything has its own time, place, and duration

10 yet all of the lifeforce that manifests in our
      experience
   comes from an earth
   with heaven standing at its center

11 as we stand in the middle of it
   it is best that we acquiesce to the truth of it
   as well as the truth of our own humanity

12 holding life in this manner reveals the simplicity of
      the best
   approach

13 pattern your way of living after the *tao* source of
      life and you will
   begin to perceive it
   and it will shape you accordingly

14 guide your life with the strength and character of
      the *tao* source of
   life
   and it will be directed accordingly

15 but allow confusion into your life and you will be
      disassociated
   accordingly

16 proper alignment with the *tao* way of life
   begets resonance with the *tao* source of life

17 proper alignment with the strength and character
      of the *tao* source of
   life
   begets resonance with the character of the *tao*
      way of life

18 alignment with confusion begets dissonance with
      both the path and
   its characteristics
   it is at this point you will be separated from the
      middle position
   you will be lost between heaven and earth

CHAPTER TWENTY-THREE

COMMENTARY

1 MIND: Demonstrations of clever thinking or pedantic intellectualism, for its own sake, are forms of materialism that disrupts authentic intuitive comprehension of life and the Tao.

2 BODY: Moderate speech in tone, volume and content does not disrupt the connection to the Tao Source.

3 BODY: Speech that is loud, aggressive, irrational, or intrusive disrupts the connection to the Tao Source of both the speaker and the listener.

4–5 BODY: Intrusive speech damages the health of the bodymind, specifically the kidneys and the *dantien* (lower Heaven).

6 BODY and HEART: To the Taoist, the universe is a fundamentally optimistic and loving place. In archaic Taoist language, the word "Tao" has a host of meanings, including nature, speech, love, words, action, and silence, among others.

7-8 BODY and HEART: The authentic Tao is heard in silence, felt in solitude, and seen in stillness.

9 MIND: Tao nature, in this case, is the power of creativity and the human drive to create. Taoists see mankind as the creative force on the planet. This drive to create sustains and holds all of nature together. Without humanity expressing itself creatively, the heavens and the earth would cease to exist. There is a natural cycle to creative pursuits that must include periods of rest and repose.

10 MIND: Nourishing *qi* energy comes to us as a result of a natural balance that hinges upon our perception of our place and purpose in the universe.

11-12 MIND: If you see yourself as explained in stanzas 9 and 10, your individual path to the Tao Source will manifest mystically.

13 HEART and BODY: If the Taoist Cultivator follows the path as it is mystically revealed then the Tao Way of Life will shape and change them. It is important to note that Taoists strive to meet life as it comes and on its terms, rather than forcing it to conform to their own preconceived plans and ideas.

14 HEART and BODY: An authentic life is one guided by the Tao Source. Nothing of worth can be accomplished without a connection to the Tao Source.

15 HEART and BODY: Confusion and disorder are anathema to the Taoist Cultivator whose job it is to observe the rhythm and flow of life.

16–18 HEART and BODY: This alignment is philosophic, energetic, intellectual, physical, and behavioral. The middle place is a reaffirmation of the optimal posture of humanity. This position forms the linchpin that holds all of existence together.

CHAPTER TWENTY-FOUR

1 if you become lost between heaven and earth

2 you will have no root
   you will have no core
   you will have no motive force
   you will have no lifeforce to extend into living

3 you will not be luminous
   you will not be able to ingest life
   you will not be able to think properly
   you will not be able to see clearly

4 showing yourself off
   seeing yourself as always correct
   passing off information as knowledge
   forcing your ideas on others
   disturbing the peace of another person's home

5 these are all symptoms of a cancerous existence
   in which your heart spirit is not straight
   it is like an arrow shot into the sky
   and lost forever

6   these are distortions and misrepresentations of the
        virtuous truth of
    the *tao* way of life
    these are distortions and misrepresentations of the
        virtuous reasons
    for living the the *tao* way of life

7   they are repugnant to us all
    so we avoid them

COMMENTARY

1 MIND: Becoming lost between Heaven and Earth is the result of a life led that has no coherent connection to the Tao Source. This is a common spiritual ailment that results from living an unauthentic life. Taoist Cultivators perfected numerous methods to remedy this situation.

2 MIND: "Root" refers to a firm terrestrial connection, "core" refers to a condensed reservoir of life-force energy, "motive force" is a drive to action, and "life-force to extend" is *qi* that flows from deep within.

3 MIND: "Luminous" is a glowing countenance. "Ingest life" means to absorb the *qi* of life as you meet it. To "think properly" refers to reasoning clearly with regard to higher ideals. "See clearly" refers to intuitive insight.

4 BODY and MIND: This type of behavior invariably results when one is lost between Heaven and Earth.

5 HEART: Describes a life led without purpose.

6–7 **HEART:** Taoists positively affect the world around them by personally cultivating the Tao Way of Life. However, behaving like a Taoist in the absence of a real connection to the Tao Source can only bring harm to a community.

CHAPTER TWENTY-FIVE

1   the ancient child asks
what is it that is beyond opposites and extremes

2   to stand upright amid the *tao* source of life

3   the ancient child asks
how does one do this

4   stand upright and alone
amidst the chaotic commerce
reveal the mysterious channel of unlimited capacity
with neutral will and intention

5   distant mind   ever surprised
distant thought   ever alert
distant traveler   ever aware

6   feel the opened space that
exists before and between
heaven and earth

7   be spontaneously silent, quiet, still, and dynamic
to gain admittance

8 be naturally isolated, random, genuine, and
     perennial
  to fuse with the changing changelessness and
     space
  that is your ever-present womb, home, and
     companion

9 from this place
  you stand
  for this space is the door and source
  from which existence flows
  and makes itself known to you

10 though invisible to me and unnamed
  I sense its presence
  by its shadow and tracks as it moves through me
  and I through it

11 it is a private experience
  intimate in the extreme and latent in antithesis

12 so I call it the *tao* way of life even as my words
     evaporate

13 domesticated people cannot perceive its real name
  for its name is a word enfolding
  miraculous power
  stalwart power
  constant power
  great power

14 the great is sufficient in itself
for addressing
that which is so close
yet
so far away

15 that which is separated
yet
intensely unified

16 that which comes closer to you
as it moves further away

17 in this greatness the *tao* source of life turns on
the whim of intention
yet
is affected by nothing
sufficient unto itself and its reflections

18 the *tao* source of life is great from above
heaven as creation is great
earth as receptive is great
man in his humanity is great

19 *tao* source of life
heaven as creation
earth as receptive
man in his humanity

20 all are great
and that's all we can normally see

and we are part of it
as it is part of us

21 man in his humanity is guided by the receptive
earth

22 receptive earth is guided by heaven as creation

23 heaven as creation is guided by the *tao* source of life

24 the *tao* source of life is wrapped in the self-formed
gossamer of
spontaneous force
that exists of its own accord

COMMENTARY

*This entire chapter consists of specific instructions for
Taoist cultivation.*

1 **HAND:** The Taoist Master channels Lao-tzu. Being
beyond opposites and extremes means employing
Taoist techniques of cultivating balance and
equilibrium in thought, word, and deed. In other
words, the Middle Path.

2 HAND: This is Taoism in a nutshell. Cultivation techniques are often explained with great concision.

3 HAND: During direct transmission of the Classic, the student's depth of understanding is judged by the completeness and sophistication of the instructions extrapolated from the standard text.

4 HAND: These are instructions. The Mysterious Channel in Taoist archaic language has several meanings: **a)** the *qi* circuits known as the Governor Vessel and Conceptual Vessel, **b)** the *qi* circuit known as the Central Vessel, or **c)** the totality of the life-force anatomy of the Cultivator's bodymind as it connects to the Tao Source.

5 HAND: Along with neutral will and intention, this stanza describes the mental state of the Cultivator that serves as a backdrop to the following meditation technique.

6 HAND: These are meditation instructions.

7 HAND: Spontaneity, or *tzu-jan*, is a fundamental Taoist concept. It forms the warp and woof of the sacred open space.

8 HAND and BODY: The rules of Taoist meditation and the rules for Taoist living are the same.

9 HAND: The Taoist Cultivator becomes a conduit for the power of the Tao Source.

10–12 MIND and HAND: Words are not absolute and cannot define the Absolute. The experience of the Absolute must be a private one.

13–16 MIND: A description of the Tao Source of Life.

17 HEART: Intention, in this case, must be authentic and spontaneous.

18–20 MIND: We are a vital part of the Tao and always have been. Heaven's greatness is seen in its outpouring, and Earth's greatness is seen in its ability to receive that outpouring. Man's greatness is seen in his ability to exist within the outpouring, channeling its force without interference.

21–24 MIND: The planet informs Humanity while the heavens inform planet Earth. The heavens are informed by the Tao Source. The Tao Source is eternal.

CHAPTER TWENTY-SIX

1. the ancient child asks
   but where can you find the connection

2. it is a bright moment that cannot be grasped

3. gravity intelligence must have an earth center
   to find its core
   and bring auspicious stability
   to those quarters shallow
   and not yet complete

4. as foundation and embodied root
   gravity intelligence
   secures profundity in the unprofound

5. for the planet on which we stand
   and its wonders all around us
   are both our model and our entry point
   to the concentration of impervious integrity

6. the wise traveler
   as gentle soul
   is a man reserved and understated
   who moves over the land cheerfully

7 carrying the weight of his own existence
   as a cherished memory forever near

8 only softly at rest and true repose
   can he visit the honest gravity intelligence

9 of his own existence
   and rejuvenate himself
   for journeys anew

10 but what motivates someone to retain a sense of
         humor
   about themselves
   while showing true concern for the hearts, minds,
         and lives
   of people they have never met

11 the only answer is the selfsame gravity intelligence

12 if you have a firm root and core
   born of its honest weight
   then you will not lose your foundation
   life's movement will then be deliberate and unhurried
   and will
   itself
   protect you

COMMENTARY

1 MIND: This question and answer is crucial in determining the student's grasp of Taoist mind-science.

2 MIND: The true connection to the Tao Source is elusive and reveals itself to the Cultivator during meditation. The Cultivator experiences it as a flash of light or flame that appears on the edge of conscious awareness.

3 HEART: "Gravity intelligence," or *chung*, is Taoist archaic language for the seed of realization. This seed, experienced as a flash of light, vanishes if the Cultivator focuses on it. If, however, the Cultivator treats it casually, then it stabilizes and grows. Eventually, it ushers in a profound awakening.

4 MIND: Under the influence of *chung* the Cultivator is able to perceive the profound depths of any object or event that is encountered—to see the heart, origin, and outcome of experiential reality.

5 MIND: An affinity or appreciation for nature is vital to securing the seed of realization.

6-10 BODY: These stanzas describe how the Taoist lifestyle supports formal cultivation practices like meditation. The entire art of Taoist cultivation is designed to engender and maintain a firm connection to the Tao Source of Life. A meditation practice that does not spill over into everyday life is fundamentally worthless. Likewise, a lifestyle that does not support meditation practice is also worthless. The implications of this world view can become so overwhelming and imposing that beginning Cultivators often lose heart and fall off the path. To remedy this, the Cultivator must learn to maintain a sense of humor about, what is ultimately, a very serious practice. Simply put, a Cultivator must learn to relax and treat the whole affair casually.

11 MIND: The seed of realization, when held casually, imbues the Cultivator with a sense of profound physical, mental, and emotional comfort, as well as an elevated level of compassion for others.

12 MIND and HEART: An alternate translation might be:

> if you can draw energy from the earth and gather it within you
>
> without over-thinking about or fixating on the seed of realization
>
> then you won't retard cultivation practice or lose what you have gained

146

you will experience your life as deliberate,
    unhurried and free from worry
and the normal ebb and flow
of your day to day existence
will comfort you and support your connection to
    the *tao* source.

二十七

CHAPTER TWENTY-SEVEN

1　the ancient child asks
　　how should you walk

2　I should walk as if each step
　　is touched by nature
　　and does not disturb the *tao* way of living

3　the ancient child asks
　　how should you talk

4　I should speak with a quiet honesty
　　that issues from my core
　　like an inverted bell
　　and not disturb the peace of others

5　the ancient child asks
　　how should you see

6　I should observe the count of life with my intuition
　　that honors my memory by setting it free
　　and not rely on the rational order of things,
　　　　objects, and quantities

7 the ancient child asks
   how should you enter doorways to infinity

8 I should regard every threshold as an entrance to
        a domain
   that protects my sense of wonder
   and guarantees a stranger's rest in a friendly land

9 the ancient child asks
   how should you join with life

10 I should bind myself to life with invisible knots
   that cannot be untied by any man
   and I should be forever bound
   and forever free

11 the ancient child asks
   should you disregard or reject people

12 no
   I should bless everyone that I meet
   and give them a gift
   even if only an earth-searching smile

13 the ancient child asks
   should you disregard or reject beneficial goods

14 no
   for everything is useful as a reflection of the *tao*
        source of life

and if I am not blinded by utility
then I will instantly know how best to employ these
    goods

15 the ancient child asks
if you follow this course
who will you be able to help

16 everyone

17 the ancient child asks
if you follow this course
who will you be able to teach

18 everyone

19 they will provide me with the tools and substance
    needed to help
and teach them

20 the ancient child asks
if they already have the tools and substance
why can't they help themselves

21 because like the emperors and empresses of
    mankind
they have looked
and ceased to see

22 having become enamored of looking and not seeing
they require a clever person
to pierce and steal the confusion
and show them the lustrous gossamer road
back to their essential nature

COMMENTARY

*Chapter Twenty-seven continues the discussion from
the previous chapter and outlines in greater detail
what it means to lead a Taoist life. It is important to note
that the Cultivator must first establish and maintain a
connection to the Tao Source and then, secondly,
awaken the seed of realization through meditation.
Thus prepared, the Cultivator attempts to shape his
behavior according to the guidelines that follow.*

*During the direct transmission of the Tao Te Ching, the
Master calls upon the student to answer direct questions
about how to conduct oneself in accordance with Taoist
precepts. The power of a verbal call and response
interrupted only by the composition and recording of
spontaneous verse with brush and ink ushers in a series
of expansions in consciousness. This cascade of
alterations in consciousness mystically reveal advanced
cultivation techniques to the student.*

1–2 **BODY:** Walk/walking: all physical movement. Nature: Mother Nature, the natural world, out of doors.

3–4 **BODY:** Talk/talking: all speech and intention to speak. Core: the lower *dantien*. Inverted bell: focused direction, speaking directly to a person.

5–6 **BODY:** Honoring memory: absolving oneself of the need to deliberately remember anything, trusting that you will rediscover or remember any information as it becomes necessary, committing something to memory by choosing not to memorize it. Rational Order: the usual, the accepted, that which is expected.

7–8 **BODY:** Threshold: gates, entrances, changes in terrain, new places. Sense of Wonder: to see through a child's eyes, to see everything as if it's the very first time. Stranger's Rest: treat everywhere you go, even familiar surroundings, as someplace totally new waiting for you to discover it.

9–10 **BODY:** Bind myself: to see oneself intimately connected to, literally, everyone and everything.

11–12 **BODY:** Bless … gift: wishing peace and comfort, yours is the hand that consecrates.

13–14 **BODY and MIND:** Utility: a reasoned usefulness or profitability to some end, preconceiving a fitness to accomplish some goal. Taoists believe that a thing can exist merely for the sake of its own existence. It need not be "useful" to have worth.

15–19 BODY: When you live according to these precepts, everyone becomes your student and your teacher. Every person that you encounter becomes the most important person in the world.

20–21 BODY and MIND: As an accident of genetics, culture, and conditioning, humanity believes itself to be made up of ordinary people seeking congress with the Tao Source. Taoists believe that they are creative expressions of the Tao Source seeking the profundity of being ordinary people. Looked and ceased to see: a bodymind clouded by illusion cannot have a complete experience of life.

22 BODY: A "clever person" is a Taoist Cultivator. "Essential nature" is your original self as an expression of the Tao Source.

ニ +)(

CHAPTER TWENTY-EIGHT

1   the ancient child asks
is this journey back to their essential nature
a journey to a far away place

2   no
the essential nature of man is all-pervasive

3   know the outflowing of lifeforce
from the three places and
strive to be the expressive quality
of the receptive earth
honoring its potential to be filled
with an understated quality of everyday life
and you will return to your essential nature

4   in this *tao* way of living
you will reclaim your innocence

COMMENTARY

1–2 HEART and MIND: The keys to reclaiming your essential nature are all around you and immediately accessible. All that is required is a mystic approach.

3 BODY, MIND, and HAND: There are three areas of the bodymind that Taoists see as points of ingress and egress for life-force energy. These are the lower *dantien* (a spot three and one-half inches below your navel and one and a half inches beneath the surface of your lower abdomen), the middle *dantien* (located just beneath the surface of your breastbone), and the upper *dantien* (located between the eyebrows above the bridge of your nose and approximately one inch beneath the surface). Collectively, these are known as the three *yao*, or positions. As a specific meditation, Cultivators envision a gentle omni-directional extension of *qi* energy from these three positions into the Cultivator's immediate environment. This extension supports and invigorates any creative human endeavor such as art, music, craft, etc.

4 BODY, MIND, and HAND: Making something for the sheer joy of making it is the Taoist path to innocence, expanded awareness, and rediscovery of your pure unspoiled self.

二十九

CHAPTER TWENTY-NINE

1   the ancient child asks
    can you control the universe by overtly grasping it
    can you shape and bend it to your will with
        outward force
    can you assert yourself over nature and truly
        control it

2   no
    the uncreated can be grasped only by not
        grasping it
    the uncreated can be willed only by an inward force
    the uncreated can be controlled only by releasing
        control
    completely

3   yes
    control by surrendering
    bend and shape through an inward willing
    passively assert through active non-assertion

4   to make it is to spoil it
    to hold it is to lose it

5 the ancient child asks
   should you interfere with the world

6 no
   to interfere with the world puts it just outside your
       reach
   you cannot succeed
   the unfolding world is a heavenly vessel which
       cannot be made
   because it already exists
   beyond desire and conception
   and always has

7 attempting to create it
   scars it
   sometimes beyond recognition

8 to make it is to spoil it
   to hold it is to lose it

9 do not interfere
   dance with it instead

10 some things go forward
   other things recede
   some things lead
   other things follow
   some things blow hot
   other things blow cold
   some are strong
   others are weak

some things are separate
other things come together
some things stand
other things fall

COMMENTARY

Fewer than seventy Chinese characters are used to transmit the knowledge in Chapter Twenty-nine. The Master reveals them in random groups to the student, who must intuitively assemble them in correct order. Along the way, the student must demonstrate calligraphically and verbally that he understands the concept of Non-assertion of the Uncreated.

1–2 **HEART:** This chapter is sometimes called the Treatise on the Non-Assertion of the Uncreated. It outlines the manner in which the Cultivator and the Tao Source become full partners in the manifestation and shaping of the phenomenal world. Taoists believe that this partnership is humanity's birthright. The "uncreated" in stanza two refers to the field of all possibility; the very substance of creation that sits at the heart of everything that exists.

3–4 HEART: The Master who speaks for Lao-tzu during the transmission delivers this statement.

5–8 HEART: Noninterference with the order and function of the natural world is a fundamental Taoist precept. That having been said, Taoists also feel that they can make suggestions to the phenomenal universe via the Tao Source. The secrets to allowing these suggestions to change and shape the world as we experience it are contained in these stanzas.

9 HEART and MIND: Noninterference is the Taoist way. Dancing implies cooperation between dance partners where each reads the motion and nuance of the other. In this context, it also implies that the partners must surrender a part of their own individuality to the dance itself.

10 MIND: The demonstration of opposites is a common Taoist method of using extremes to explain not only the flux and flow of the universe but also the point of dynamic equilibrium between the two. Aligning oneself with this equilibrium is a primary goal of cultivation.

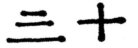

CHAPTER THIRTY

1   the ancient child asks
    who can help

2   anyone

3   the ancient child asks
    who can help you

4   everyone

5   the ancient child asks
    how can you help them

6   by showing them how to be resolute

7   the ancient child asks
    how can they help you

8   by learning to be resolute

9   the ancient child asks
    what is resolute

10 not violent
not arrogant
not boastful
not haughty
not weak
not obsequious

11 the ancient child asks
why must they be resolute

12 because there is no other way to enter the *tao*
source of life

13 the ancient child asks
who acts with resolve and determination

14 a good man
who protects his essential nature and abhors
unwise force
but acts when it is time to act
acts resolutely
stops and withdraws

COMMENTARY

1–2 BODY: Anyone you meet as you go through life can help you along the Tao Path, as you see yourself in others.

3–4 BODY: In reality, everyone has something to teach, even if they teach it unknowingly.

5–6 BODY and HEART: The Taoist Cultivator leads by example. *Kuo*, or resoluteness, forms the base of Taoist character. It has several meanings, including: is resolved, has firm resolution, brings results, achieves goals, fulfills purpose, and generates effects.

7–8 BODY: The best way to help people be the best that they can be is for you to be the very best that you can be.

9–10 BODY: These stanzas define the six qualities of resoluteness.

11–12 BODY: Someone who does not follow the six qualities of resoluteness cannot maintain a strong connection with the Tao Source of Life.

13–14 BODY: This is the definition of the Taoist *chung jen*, or superior man.

CHAPTER THIRTY-ONE

1 the ancient child asks
violence
is it resolute

2 no

3 the ancient child asks
is it just

4 no

5 the ancient child asks
if I project violence outward what will happen

6 it comes back to me

7 the ancient child asks
can a violent man be fine-spun

8 no

9 the ancient child asks
can a violent man find the *tao*

10 no

11 the ancient child asks
   who made this sword

12 a man

13 the ancient child asks
   was the man who made this sword fine-spun

14 yes
   if it is a good sword
   yes

15 fine-spun man
   fine-spun sword
   together they ride the winds
   move the heavens
   and rule the earth

16 the ancient child asks
   how do they do this

17 it is a secret held in your hands

18 the ancient child asks
   when is this secret revealed

19 only when it is necessary

20 if the secret is revealed too soon it is spoiled and
     despised
   then the sword and the man are of no use to
     themselves or others

21 the ancient child asks
   where does wisdom come from

22 I hear it in my left ear
   it floats

23 the ancient child asks
   where does anger come from

24 I hear it in my right ear
   it falls hard

25 the ancient child asks
   which is fine-spun

26 the left

27 the ancient child asks
   can you force wisdom to speak to your left ear

28 no
   it speaks when it is ready
   you have to wait
   the right speaks all the time
   it is deafening

CHAPTER THIRTY-ONE

29 the ancient child asks
   how can you stop the right from speaking all the time

30 by gently
   lying down
   sitting
   standing and
   walking

31 the ancient child asks
   where does this work best for you

32 at my home where things are familiar and I
       feel safe
   anger can be stopped there with the four virtues

33 home is anywhere I can feel the *tao* beneath my feet
   my feet must be fine-spun as well

34 the ancient child asks
   what do your fine-spun feet tell you

35 do not find joy in hurting people
   if you must hurt someone
   listen to the left
   keep your heart spirit calm
   and be fine-spun
   you cannot find the *tao* source of life if you enjoy
       being violent

and hurt people, their land, and even their animals
   on the land
if you live life violently
the life around you will disappear

36 there is a time to be happy and a time to be sad
know how to differentiate between the two so you
   know where to
lie
sit
stand
walk
if you cultivate these virtues you will be happy
if someone is hurt be sad
treat it like a funeral
because an opportunity to enter the *tao* has died

COMMENTARY

1–2 **HEART and MIND:** "Violence" refers to unnatural
force, to overpower, to dominate, force, compel, or to
employ your gifts and strengths in an unnatural manner.

3–4 **HEART and MIND:** "Just" means auspicious,
generating a beneficial outcome, or creating good
fortune.

5–6 HEART and MIND: Projecting violence means more than roughly dominating others. Violence can be projected even when you are alone. Thinking and intention can take on violent aspects. This disturbs the soul of the world. Taoists see this as an injury done to the Tao Source itself, which in turn injures everyone, including the person who projected the violence.

7–8 MIND: Fine-spun: wise, noble, honorable, high self-esteem, values-driven. The image of finely spun filaments describes the quality of spiritual energy that pervades the bodymind of a resolute follower of the Tao.

9–10 HEART: Plainly stated, one who forces life cannot maintain a coherent connection to the Tao Source.

11–14 MIND: The Chinese double-edged sword, or *jian*, known as the King Of Weapons, is an important Taoist icon. The skill and focus required to properly wield it mirrors the Taoist ideal of resoluteness. Ancient Chinese believed that you could judge the depths of a person's humanity by the quality of their swordplay. Likewise, a swordmaker's character can be judged by the quality of the sword. This is true for any art or craft. During the transmission of this chapter, the Master actually brandishes a live blade.

15 MIND: The double-edged sword is used by Taoist Cultivators to focus and refine the *qi*, or life-force energy, of their bodymind. It is used in meditation, *qigong*, and calligraphy practice, as well as in friendly competitions.

16-17 HAND: This is a reference to the Secret Sword Hand Mudra, a hand formation held during meditation that subtly affects and deepens the meditative state. It is formed by bending the ring and little finger to touch the thumb and extending the index and middle fingers as if the blade of a straight sword.

18-19 HAND: Warns against attempting to focus the bodymind energies too soon. An expansive energy gathering in the palms during meditation signals the appropriate time to employ the mudra.

20 HEART and HAND: Emphasizes knowing the right time to employ a specific meditative technique or contemplative skill.

21-22 HEART: Taoist Cultivators frequently experience intuitive insights, as if someone is whispering in their left ear. The words they hear are, frequently, in their own voice and possess a buoyant quality.

23-24 HEART: In contrast to the intuitive, the rational over-thinking mind sounds like a harsh rain falling and, generally, speaks in a strange or unfamiliar voice. Cultivators experience this voice as something heard in the right ear.

25-26 MIND: This is an injunction to listen to the intuitive mind. The intuition both supports and generates resoluteness.

27-28 HEART and MIND: Intuition cannot be forced or manipulated. It must be allowed. The rational mind forces its way in to the consciousness.

29-30 HAND: These are postures for Taoist *qigong* and meditation. Engaging in these activities induces a state of quiescence that subdues the over-thinking mind and invites the intuitive mind to come forward. Lying, sitting, standing, and walking are called the Four Virtues. Each represents a body of cultivation technique that grants the Cultivator access to their innermost self.

31-32 HAND and BODY: *Qigong* and meditation should be performed in comfortable, safe, and, preferably, familiar surroundings.

33-35 HAND and MIND: Refers to a blending of the bodymind's life-force with the *qi* of the planet. During this activity, the *qi* of the Earth enters the Cultivator in pulsating waves that comfort the Cultivator and dramatically stimulates the intuition. Taoists call this meditation Listening to the Primal Mother.

36 HEART and MIND: Choosing the right time and place to meditate or play *qigong* is a fundamental skill that each Cultivator must learn. This is a delicate proposition. Choosing the wrong time or place can actually harm the Cultivator.

CHAPTER THIRTY-TWO

1 the *tao* source of life is vast and unlimited
the *tao* source of life is beyond ordinary reason
   and logic
the *tao* source of life is unfathomable and
   unnamable
it is beyond words and labels
it is beyond deliberateness

2 the ancient child asks
why can't you grasp it

3 because it's too big and too small at the same time
because it is one thing and many things at the
   same instant
and you cannot divide it into parts
it cannot be held or known on purpose

4 utility is useful for only a short time

5 these are instructions

6 lie down
sit

stand
walk in a deliberate manner
allow heaven into your bodymind
draw the earth into your bodymind
let them mingle around the center of your bodymind
resisting the desire to command or control
it will feel like a gentle rain is falling within and
    without you
swallow the saliva like it was honey
that condenses like a sweet dew into your core
and rest peacefully and naturally within the *tao*
    source of life
knowing that its heartbeat
is your own

7 the heartbeat will shape, carve, and form you into
    what is needed
at this moment in space and time and no more

8 do not be in a hurry for the future
rather allow the unnamed to flow into the named
    to reveal the
present ever

9 embodying balance, poise, and equilibrium
you will have no difficulty seeing
you are a part of a vast undifferentiated whole
you are a swirling eddy in the great river
you are a drop of water in the great ocean

10 despite what your dividing mind says
   remind yourself
   that you are always home

COMMENTARY

1–4 **HEART and MIND:** These stanzas restate the Taoist idea that the Tao Source is beyond analysis and reason. It is unknowable in the conventional sense. In effect, the Tao Source of Life can only be understood in the aftermath of a purposefully engineered accident. Consequently, Taoists will arrange their lives and endeavors to accommodate those accidents.

5–6 **HAND:** An alternate translation might be:
   lie down with mindful awareness
   sit erect with mindful awareness
   stand in a balanced and poised posture
   walk with full awareness of each step
   envision the power of the heavens flowing down
      through the crown of your head
   envision the power of the planet flowing up
      through the bodymind as it contacts the earth
   suggest the energies to mix and blend together at
      a spot three and one-half inches below your

navel and inward. (lower dantien)

do not attempt to control or influence the progress of the blending; merely watch it occur

imagine that there is a gentle summer rain falling on you

swallow your saliva as it builds up in your closed mouth

imagine that this health-giving elixir collects in your lower dantien

remain peaceful, calm, and relaxed

you will begin to feel a pulsating within your bodymind

this pulsating is a natural occurrence that you should neither encourage nor restrain.

7–8 MIND: Do not try to understand what is occurring or become impatient regarding an outcome. Simply let it happen.

9 HAND and MIND: The Taoist reality holds that each person is a vital part of the Tao, but we have, over time, forgotten this fact. The result is a less-than-complete experience of our life and world. Taoist philosophy and cultivation seeks to remedy this situation.

10 MIND: A reminder that we are all part of the Tao Source.

CHAPTER THIRTY-THREE

1   focus and forget

2   learn to understand the outside world by looking
        inward
    and you will access true and authentic wisdom
    learn to understand the inside world by looking
        outward
    and you will access true and authentic knowledge

3   when true and authentic wisdom and true and
        authentic knowledge
    intermingle, you will see
    wise force at work and know how to employ it

4   control the useful parts with it
    control the border between the inside world and
        the outside world
    with it

5   be aware, alert, and relaxed as you are the crux
        of the moment

6   the *tao* will take you by surprise
flame, light, fog, and cloud appear
as boundaries are dissolved
and senses burned away

7   employ wise force to manage the moment
deliver confusion to the earth
rest comfortably
weep if you must but only in joyousness
and you will secure a silent and gentle victory

8   the *tao* source of life reaches out for you as you
      reach out for it
effortlessly flow into one another
feel the divine force spinning and oscillating to
      and from every quarter
and be content to know that
the plan upon which all of the universe is built
is perfect and complete
benevolent and giving

9   we have all that we require

10 protect the moment with the will, thought, and
      imagination
project yourself boldly in space and time
as you fortify all that has preceded it

11 remember where you are

12 remember where you came from

13 remember your significance as a facet of the *tao*
      source of life

14 you are everlasting

15 you cannot die within the *tao* source of life

COMMENTARY

1 **HAND:** These are meditation instructions. The
meditator brings attention to the object of meditation
for a specified period of time and then releases
attention on the object and moves onto another object.

2 **HAND and MIND:** Meditate by turning inward.
Taoists believe that the external world can best be
explored, examined, and understood by exploring and
examining the inner world of the individual. The inverse
is also true. Employing this method of investigation
yields transcendental knowledge and profound wisdom.

3 **MIND:** As authentic knowledge and wisdom
appear within the consciousness of the Cultivator, a
subtle mystical strength manifests called "wise force."

4 **MIND:** Wise force is employed to deepen the Taoist mystical experience. Specific information as to implementing wise force is intuitively revealed to each Cultivator according to his or her individual needs.

5 **HAND and MIND:** These are instructions to help the Cultivator manage the deepening contemplative experience.

6 **HAND and MIND:** These are the effects of this meditation. They begin rather abruptly, giving the Cultivator a mild start. The meditator enters a reality construct in which flame, light, fog, and/or clouds envelope them. Accompanying these images is a perception that their corporeal limits begin to disappear and their primary sense organs begin to shut down.

7 **HAND and MIND:** Allow any fears, worries, uncomfortable feelings, or waves of emotion to drain downward toward the earth. Do not disturb the meditation by attempting to suppress any of these. Completion of this phase of the meditation is verified by a feeling that can be described as a subtle conquering of the moment.

8 **HAND and MIND:** This is a description of the contemplative experience as the Taoist Cultivator succeeds in resting comfortably amid the changes in consciousness.

9 HEART: This is a fundamental Taoist precept.

10 HAND: These are intermediate meditative instructions.

11–15 HAND and HEART: These are specific instructions for closing the meditation revealed in this chapter. They insure a normalizing of bodymind function and a smooth return to consensus reality.

CHAPTER THIRTY-FOUR

1   the ancient child asks
how does it feel

2   the great *tao* source of life floats and drifts
it is a candle in a room filled with mirrors
it is a diamond in a room filled with candles and
      mirrors

3   the great *tao* source of life flows and undulates
it is a spider's web that stretches in every direction
it is wondrously expansive and cyclical and unique

4   the great *tao* source of life has a rhythm to it
it revolves and spins in every direction
it connects and binds all things with freedom and
      independence
and interdependence

5   when you are aware of all these things
a light and sensitive energy collects at your crown
and space and time literally break apart

6 usual becomes unreality
reality becomes unusual

7 everything depends on this
it always has
it always will be

8 name it paint it sing it if you must
but trust it as silence
a blank canvas in the unnamed

9 it cannot die
neither can you

10 if you remain humble and quiet a new mind will
be born
where puzzles are solved in their own space and
time
where unique thinking that is greater than thought
flows like water
where flowing into human life
transforms human life

11 then you will be a great sage wise man

COMMENTARY

1–6 HAND, MIND, and HEART: Chapter Thirty-four continues the exposition of the meditative experience ushered in by the technique detailed in the previous chapter. The student actually engages this meditative technique during the direct transmission of the *Tao Te Ching*. During this process, the Master observes the student's breathing and body temperature, and also reads the pulse in the manner of a doctor of Traditional Chinese Medicine. Any and all changes in the student's energetic physiology are noted. The Master will interrupt the meditation at specific intervals and ask the student to compose spontaneous verse about what the student is experiencing. They will also engage in a complex game of call and response as a means of further suspending the rational mind and deeply imprinting the classic in the student's mind.

7 HEART: Maintaining a coherent and direct connection to the Tao Source is vital to the survival of humanity.

8 HAND: Creatively expressing this connection helps to fortify it.

9 **MIND:** The literal impossibility of death.

10–11 **HAND and MIND:** The birth of the New Mind is a seminal event in the Taoist mystical life. This "mind" has its own rules and laws. Once learned, the New Mind begins to spiritually transform the Cultivator, imbuing him with great wisdom, perspective, and insight that flow from the Tao Source.

CHAPTER THIRTY-FIVE

1   hold and embody

2   be the one who will hold and embody the *tao* way
      of life
    by shaping yourself with the great ultimate symbol
    by holding yourself within the confluence of its
      meeting rhythms
    be the one who centers themselves between
      heaven and earth

3   and move about in the field of unlimited possibilities

4   you will breathe with your skin
    you will shine with every breath

5   and quicken the way you lay, sit, stand, and walk

6   this is the true breathing that inspires and attracts
      true life
    this is the true breathing that inspires and attracts
      the *tao* source of
    life

7 each breath is an illumination
there are many illuminations

8 the ancient child asks
what follows
what flows in and flows out

9 sturdy comfort
abundant rest
organized serenity
and a smile

10 a silent song of the sweetest music
a sweet taste of honey swallowed gently
a desire to play, dance, paint, and sing

11 I am actually singing in a world that is somehow
bigger
brighter
funnier
more wondrous than I could have possibly
imagined
I want to reach out to strangers and passersby
I want to visit with them
I want to talk with them
I want to laugh with them

12 the ancient child asks
are these ghosts or real people

13 it doesn't matter

14 complete the ritual
   draw the words in a ghost's sandbox
   don't stop until it's time
   your guests want you to complete the contract
   remember
   you stand between heaven and earth
   you are the middle place

15 the ancient child asks
   can you feel my hand on your spine

16 yes I can
   my spine is part of a roof that protects me

17 the ancient child says
   yes it is
   paint the changes you feel in your spine
   show me where life rushes into you
   show me where life rushes out

18 I paint the symbols
   heaven, earth, wind, water, mountain, fire,
       thunder, and lake

19 the ancient child asks
   what do you see

20 I see a circle of jade

21 the ancient child asks
   what do you hear

22 I hear a woman singing

23 the ancient child asks
   where are you

24 I am in a church or a temple

25 the ancient child asks
   what color is the road outside

26 it is blue-green

27 the ancient child asks
   what are you doing now

28 I am rocking back and forth
   I cannot stop
   and my hair is tickling me

29 the ancient child asks
   what are your emotions

30 I feel anxious
   your hand is hot on my back

31 the ancient child says
   think of a warm waterfall
   focus on your brush and continue to paint

32 my family is all sitting around a table reading
      and talking

CHAPTER THIRTY-FIVE

33 the ancient child asks
   is the table upstairs or downstairs

34 our dining room is upstairs

35 the ancient child asks
   what do you see

36 a bowl of fruit in the center

37 the ancient child asks
   where are you

38 I am on a farm

39 the ancient child asks
   what time of year is it

40 it is my birthday

41 these places cannot be seen or heard
   these places are innumerable and inexhaustible
         and subtle
   you have the power to go to any of these places
   if you will but return there often
   visit, commune, and rest there
   don't speak of them
   because words as drugs and words as labels are
         coarse
   they will rob them of their real taste

42 instead
   simply
   remember

43 return home

COMMENTARY

1–2 HAND: These are *qigong* instructions. The Taoist Cultivator performs physical movements that trace the shape of the Grand Ultimate Diagram, or *T'ai Chi Tu.* More commonly this is known as the *yin* and *yang.*

Taoist Cultivators believe that moving in the shape of the *yin* and *yang* brings them closer to the mysteries that it represents. Taoists say that they enter the mystery through its shape.

3 HAND: Early Taoist *qigong* had few rules and restrictions. Basically, the player engineers a state of quiescence and creates a freeform movement sequence within the limiting structure of the *yin* and *yang* shape. To create movement that represents the interplay of cosmic forces while moving in circles within circles yields an intensity that transforms the bodymind.

4 **HAND:** Under the influence of authentic *qigong* the Cultivator feels as though he is breathing through the pores of his skin. An inhalation generates a feeling of sucking air inwardly through the skin. During an exhalation, the Cultivator experiences an omni-directional expansion of life-force energy exuding from the bodymind.

5–6 **MIND:** This kind of breathing is called True Breathing. It consolidates and intensifies the *qi* of the bodymind.

7 **MIND:** Taoists believe that the seed of awakening exists at the core of every breath.

8 **MIND:** At this point the Master, channeling Lao-tzu, begins to judge the depth of the student's mystical experience.

9–11 **HEART:** This is one of the more personal moments to occur during Direct Transmission. The student's answers during the call and response reveal important information about the psyche of the student. In addition, clues to intermediate and advanced cultivation bubble up in the form of archetypal images.

12–13 **HEART:** Occasionally, students have visions of strangers as well as people from their past.

14 HAND: The ghost sandbox is sometimes called a *fu-kay*, or Spirit Board. It is a two- to three-foot square table. The edges of the table are raised so as to accommodate a layer of red sand. During intermediate and advanced meditation, the student experiences cascading visions of esoteric Chinese characters that are not in common usage. The student writes them in the surface of the red sand with an awl made of peach-wood, and the Master interprets the meaning of each. Taoist Priests use this table to communicate with the spirits of the dead.

15–16 HAND: The Master will often extend his own life-force energy into the bodymind of the student during direct transmission. In this case, *qi* was extended into the area between the student's kidneys as a way of boosting the student's overall vitality. This insures that the mystic visions continue until they naturally stop.

17–18 HAND: The student uses brush and ink to express the flux and flow of life-force energy in his bodymind.

19–20 HAND, MIND, and HEART: A circle of jade appearing in the consciousness of the student is a primary Taoist image. Its appearance signals a major spiritual accomplishment.

21–22 HAND, MIND, and HEART: Likewise, the perceived sound of a woman singing signifies a momentous mystical event.

23–28 HAND, MIND, and HEART: All of the images revealed in these stanzas arise spontaneously and vary slightly from Cultivator to Cultivator. The experience of each is so profound that they become imprinted on the memory of the Cultivator and remain among the most vivid and visceral events of the Taoist's life. These responses are of a highly personal and intimate nature.

29–30 HAND, MIND, and HEART: The Master monitors the student's emotions throughout the direct transmission. This is all part of the process of judging the quality and depth of the mystic experience.

31–40 HAND: As the mystic process continues to unfold, the student is constantly required to express personal reflections and emotions calligraphically. This is similar to automatic writing in the Western tradition. Contained in these bursts of calligraphy are advanced cultivation instructions that appear from unknown quarters.

41–43 HAND, MIND, and HEART: A sacred precinct forms at the end of the string of visions. This is a mystical place that, according to Taoist cosmology, exists in a dimension parallel to our own. This dimension becomes a sanctum to the Cultivator. Returning to it replenishes and nourishes the Cultivator.

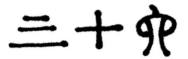

CHAPTER THIRTY-SIX

1   the ancient child says
     to see the future
     put your left hand over your breast bone
     and look into your right palm

2   rotate your fist as if gathering yarn left and right
     expand yourself to every quarter
     until you feel the orbiting movements of the planets
        within you

3   draw an imaginary gossamer bow and shoot an
        arrow
     left and right

4   the ancient child asks
     but what are arrows

5   arrows are wishes and thought forms

6   weak at rest
     strong in motion

7   they will find their mark
    if the archer is calm, focused, and controlled

8   the ancient child asks
    how do you condense your bodymind, spirit, and
        lifeforce

9   collect yourself to your core center
    by reaching out with your bodymind
    in order to go definitely inward
    you must definitely reach outward

10 the ancient child asks
    how do you condense your bodymind and spirit
        and lifeforce

11 reach out with your bodymind and support the
        heavens above you
    using absolutely no strength at all

12 keep your five fingers open if you want to grasp
        silver and gold

13 the ancient child asks
    how can this be
    what is the secret

14 it is a game without a winner
    you are both contestants
    it is a joyous dance

you are both dancers
it is a puppet show
you are the marionette and the hands
    manipulating strings

15 each of us is subtle and hidden away
revealed only by the true breath

16 out reaching
out shining

17 both are allowed to happen because
the *tao* way of life can never be forced
it can only be invited in

18 the voice of the wonderwork is subtle and hidden
    away
you must be quiet and still to hear it clearly

19 the light of the wonderwork is subtle and hidden
    away
you must move about mysteriously and make tiny
    adjustments
in your bodymind to see it clearly

20 the substance of the wonderwork is subtle and
    hidden away
you must touch and caress it by letting it touch and
    caress you

CHAPTER THIRTY-SIX

21 the taste of the wonderwork is subtle and hidden
away
you must turn your tongue in an empty mouth to
savor it

22 the aroma of the wonderwork is subtle and hidden
away
you must rely on afterthoughts, memories, and
musings to reveal its
smell

23 silent victory
quietly conquering

24 this is how you should behave

25 that is the secret

26 the ancient child asks
can you not see it clearly
are you a fish stubbornly dying on the dry shore
refusing to enter the ocean
until you understand it clearly

27 the ancient child asks
is there anything to be gained by killing yourself

28 there is nothing to be gained by suicide

29 the ancient child says
   use the natural gifts you have to explore
   your inner world

30 after all
   it's a sin to ignore your talents

31 do you think that your talents are for showing off

COMMENTARY

1 **HAND:** This is a meditative posture designed to stimulate the intuition. Ancient Taoists used it to divine the future. The psychological implications of the pose are numerous. The Chinese character *pi* in this stanza literally means "to gently place ones hand over the heart."

2 **HAND:** This is a specific *qigong* activity.
a. First, the Cultivator forms loose fists with both hands and slowly traces circles, alternately, left and right. The number of the rotations—thirty-six to each side—gathers, fortifies, and equalizes the *qi* of the bodymind.
b. The Cultivator imagines that his bodymind, now filled with balanced life-force energy, expands outward to encompass the entire universe.

c. The Cultivator maintains this identification with the expanse and void of the universe until he feels localized energy moving in cyclical patterns within the bodymind. Nurturing these patterns, referred to as "orbits," is an important part of Taoist cultivation.

3 HAND: The Cultivator mimics the motions of drawing a bow and arrow during an inhalation. As they exhale, they release the imaginary arrow and pretend to watch it as it vanishes into the distance.

4–7 MIND: Mental instructions for the *qigong* activity.

8–9 HEART and MIND: Collecting yourself confidently before you speak or act is an important Taoist ideal. These stanzas state the importance of reaching out into the world around you as a means of clarifying your inner gifts and talents. Compassion, helping others, and basic human contact are, therefore, keys to realizing your full potential.

10–12 HAND: These are *qigong* instructions in which the hands are literally held above the head as if supporting the sky. The Cultivator enters a meditative state and pretends to be solely responsible for supporting the sky above the surface of the earth. This activity naturally consolidates life-force energy to the lower *dantien* and the middle *dantien*.

13–14 MIND and BODY: Describes the mental state and psychological stance of the Cultivator.

15–16 HEART and HAND: The True Breath is described in the previous chapter.

17 HEART, MIND, and HAND: Make yourself a fit receptacle for the Tao.

18–22 HEART, MIND, and HAND: The meanings of these stanzas are subtle and complex. Essentially, they provide instructions on how to outline the force and function of the Tao Source so the Cultivator may better understand how to lead a Taoist lifestyle.

23–25 MIND and BODY: Steady progress fortified by optimism and self-confidence is the hallmark of a Taoist life.

26–28 HEART and MIND: Warns Cultivators against the trap of thinking that the *Tao* should be understood intellectually before embracing it. This is spiritual suicide.

29–30 HEART and HAND: We receive our gifts and our deficits from the Tao Source. Those gifts and deficits are, in reality, our keys to unlocking the secrets of the universe.

31 MIND: Fundamentally, our individual talents and how we exercise them are private affairs that exist for our own growth and development.

CHAPTER THIRTY-SEVEN

1   the *tao* source of life as a
    ceaseless and everlasting universal force
    is oblique

2   and never does any single thing
    yet always does every single thing

3   hold this idea firmly in your mind
    and your body will naturally align
    with the universal force

4   senses and consciousness will turn inward
    and your whole being will rest peacefully
    while
    your pure and elegant nature spontaneously
    fills you up
    denying purchase to all confusion and
        unnaturalness

5   this is how you transform yourself
    by anchoring yourself amidst the flow
    of a sea of lifeforce

6   by tranquilly sitting between
    heaven and earth

7   by turning around and listening
    to your soul

COMMENTARY

1–2 HEART and MIND: Paradoxical in nature as
well as slightly out of phase with normal perception
and understanding.

3 HAND and MIND: The basic Taoist mental stance.
Once this stance is assumed, it changes the
Cultivator's physiology.

4 HAND and MIND: The results of the basic Taoist
mental stance.

5–6 HAND, BODY and HEART: These are specific
meditative instructions designed to draw out great
wisdom from your innermost self. Taoists call this
communing with your spirit, or *shen*.

7 MIND and HEART: The soul is constantly sending
you all of the wisdom you require to establish a more
coherent connection with the Tao Source.

CHAPTER THIRTY-EIGHT

1   the ancient child asks
how do you turn around and listen to your soul

2   by selflessly acting with
the power of authentic benevolence

3   you cannot plan to do good works
good works can only be done naturally

4   a person who plans to be good
will have no power
and will not be authentic

5   the difference between authentic and inauthentic
is the benevolent power of your soul

6   an authentic man never acts
an authentic man has no hidden agenda
an authentic man seeks no rewards for his deeds

7   an inauthentic man tries too hard
an inauthentic man has ulterior motives
an inauthentic man constantly thinks of rewards

8 authenticity cannot be willed or proscribed
   authenticity cannot be planned or enforced

9 false manners are a sham

10 morality worn like a coat gives rise to shallowness
   that casts a shadow
   over everyone

11 rules and propriety arise from this darkness
   constricting the hearts and minds of humanity
   forcing their souls
   to a hiding place

12 life becomes chaotic

13 great men lecture you on your faults
   complicating simple things
   until
   they are barely recognizable

14 and you don't know which way to turn

15 but the authentic man
   allows his soul to take the lead of his life
   holds firmly to his inner truth
   gently grasping the seed of life

COMMENTARY

1–2 BODY and HAND: The Taoist spiritual goal of "turning around and listening to the soul" is accomplished via outward behavior.

3–4 BODY: Only spontaneous and naturally occurring expressions of kindness and compassion are authentic. Unauthentic expressions will not help you reach your goal.

5 MIND: The power of the soul can only be experienced through authentic expressions. In Taoist language, authentic expressions are "filled with *shen.*"

6–8 BODY and HEART: This is the crux of Taoist behavior in all public and private matters. The translation is plain enough in describing the dynamics of a deliberate and selfless lifestyle.

9–10 BODY and HEART: This is a specific criticism of Confucian ideals and a warning against going through the motions. Taoists believe that empty rituals and insincerity will, ultimately, destroy honesty and truth.

11 **BODY and HEART:** Early Taoist philosophers believed that following Confucian precepts invariably led to a stultifying societal and political correctness. These cleverly contrived patterns of acceptable behavior drained the bodymind of spirit, or *shen,* and suffocated the soul.

12 **BODY:** Whatever negatively affects the individual eventually spills out into the community at large.

13 **MIND:** Great men: clever intellectuals who revel in nuanced and complex reasoning as a way of justifying behavior; individuals who bring up ideas, oblique issues, and rationalizations in the face of spiritual truth.

14 **BODY:** The result of stifling the soul.

15 **MIND and HEART:** The Tao Source reveals inner truth via the soul. As this truth is revealed over time, the process of Taoist illumination begins to manifest.

CHAPTER THIRTY-NINE

1 authenticity
who are you
where do you reside
what sustains you
where do you go

2 I am the original bodymind
I live in the folds of essence, energy, and spirit
the *tao* way of life sustains me

3 I move about in the vast undifferentiated realm
and the field of all that is possible

4 inhale and make the sound
exhale and make the sound
and write

5

life	live	grow
full	abundance	fulfillment
divine	potent	spiritual
rest	repose	serene
pure	clear	water

6   since ancient times these have been the keys
     living and growing to an abundance of spiritual
          force and
     energized serenity acquired through tranquility

7   the pivot is a bowl of water left alone and
          undisturbed
     so the surface becomes as clear as glass
     able to reflect

8   illumination
     balance, poise, and equilibrium

9   these are the secrets of wholeness
     within the *tao* way of life

10 without the *tao* way of life
     heaven, earth, and man are divided

11 life
     fullness
     divinity
     tranquility
     clarity

12 would all be forfeit

COMMENTARY

1–2 MIND: The original bodymind expresses itself in authentic action and behavior. The roots of that authenticity reside in a precise blending of the Three Treasures:

- Essence, or *ching*: The motive force of life, radiant optimism, zest for life, personal drive, and determination. There is also a physical component of *ching* in Taoist physiology.
- Energy, or *qi*: Life-force energy, intrinsic energy, energy of creation. There is a physical component of *qi* in Taoist physiology.
- Spirit, or *shen*: The soul, the personal spirit of a human being. The *shen* bridges ordinary consciousness with the Tao Source and enters the bodymind at the time of conception. There is a physical component of *shen* in Taoist physiology.

3 MIND and HEART: A fundamental statement of Taoist empowerment.

4–5 HAND: These are instructions in mystical technique designed to demonstrate the unity of *ching*, *qi*, and *shen*. The characters in stanza 5 are each written in one continuous motion and coordinated with a single breath. Simply put, the student envisions himself afloat in the Tao Realm with his mind fixed on the character and its meaning. The student takes a deep breath while intoning the sound "*heng*" and lifts his brush above the paper. Following the inhalation, the student exhales while intoning the sound "*hah*" and draws the character. The same process is observed with each of the fifteen characters that make up the stanza.

6 **HEART:** The drawing of each character and any interplay between Master and student should not disturb the student's quiescence.

7 **MIND:** A reflective mind misses nothing of what it reflects.

8–9 **MIND and HAND:** The mystical experience of Taoist illumination must occur in a fully realized Taoist life. The three watchwords both initiate and support illumination.

10-12 **HEART:** If no one cultivated the Tao, then the goodness of the whole universe would suffer.

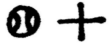

CHAPTER FORTY

1 the first step is to enter the place
from whence you came

2 the second step is to play in the field of
  limitlessness

3 the third step is to demonstrate birth, growth,
  maturation, and
death

4 the fourth step is to rest quietly
listening for wisdom and the sacred sounds
watching the web of moving existence all around
  you

5 rest
and then

6 play again

COMMENTARY

This is an important point in the direct transmission process. The student is asked to demonstrate "the interplay of being and not-being" by performing a series of transformative movements. In all three cases, I was required to engage in Taoist swordplay to reflect on the concept of "fine spun" that was introduced in Chapter Thirty-one.

Taoists regard this chapter and the activity it describes as a complete encapsulated summary of the entire Taoist philosophy. Though, as previously stated, ancient Taoists did not impose a rigid chapter structure on "Conversations with the Ancient Child," this enfolded description of Taoism usually marked the halfway point of the classic.

1 **HAND:** Ritualistically enter a sacred precinct within the Tao Realm.

2 **HAND:** Begin a series of self-directed movement improvisations driven by a mystic state.

3 **HAND:** Graphically demonstrate the natural order of the universe with movement; that is, birth (*yuan*), growth (*heng*), maturation (*li*), and death (*chen*).

4 **HAND:** Assume a meditative posture, turn inward, and maintain a state of reflective awareness.

5-6 **HAND:** After a period of reflective meditation, begin the whole process anew.

CHAPTER FORTY-ONE

1 the very best students of the *tao* way of life
try their best to be open to its mysteries
by using their higher intuition and naturally
   entering its
transcendental shape

2 they simply look
they simply see

3 the typical students of the *tao* way of life
try their best to let the mysteries in
but get in their own way by thinking into it
   too much

4 they look halfheartedly
they cannot see clearly

5 those students of the *tao* way of life that are
   worthless
cannot be said to really be students at all
because they cannot sense, see, or reason
when they hear about the mysteries

6   they laugh, ridicule, and demean the whole idea

7   what they do not realize
    is that they are only seeing
    their own blindness

8   what they do not know
    is that laughter
    is the taoist way of seeing

9   laughter outlines the great mystery

10 the ancient child asks
    what are the first qualities of a student of the *tao*
        way of life

11 higher intuition and the ability to laugh with a full
        heart

12 if you cannot laugh
    you cannot know the *tao* way of life

13 a wisdom thread that stretches back to antiquity
        tells us
    what is real and true and how to recognize it

14 the bright path seems dim
    cloudy

15 the direct path seems crooked
obscured

16 the smooth and level path
actually bobs and weaves

17 true strength of character seems weak to the
ignorant
authentic white always carries a part of blackness
with it

18 true abundance is actually empty

19 can you see it

20 the greatest stability is actually tenuous

21 can you feel it

22 the highest certitude is actually a lie

23 can you find truth that easily

24 the transcendental shape has no walls or limit

25 can you move into it

26 the transcendental shape is small and unfillable

27 can you fill it up

CHAPTER FORTY-ONE

28 the greatest talent requires time and work to ripen

29 can you patiently wait for it

30 practice does not make perfect
   practice is perfect to begin with

31 can you really behave that way

32 the greatest sound is actually silent

33 can you hear it

34 living the *tao* way of life is so ancient and natural
   that it has no name
   it is so accessible and pervasive
   that you cannot see it
   yet it is both the beginning and the end of
      everything
   that lends its profound magic to the entire world

COMMENTARY

This and the next five chapters are very important to the Cultivators of the Tao Path. They focus on personal conduct and the responsibility the Taoist has to himself as he cultivates peace and contentment. During the direct transmission, the Master delivers the verse in a dogmatic tone.

1 **BODY and MIND:** The injunction is clear; be open to the Tao Source, commune with it via your intuitive mind, and flow into it as it flows into you.

2 **BODY and MIND:** Experience life as completely as you are able.

3 **BODY and MIND:** Over-intellectualizing about the *Tao* blocks your access to it. You cannot think your way into being a Taoist. Action is required.

4 **BODY and MIND:** Over-intellectualizing reduces your ability to completely experience life.

5 **BODY and MIND:** When you cut yourself off from an authentic experience of life, you lose the ability to touch the wonders of your own existence. Your fallback position invariably results in rationalizations of your behavior that separates you further—you think so much that you lose the ability to feel.

6 **BODY and MIND:** Contemptuous laughter and behavior; to look down on.

7 **BODY and MIND:** When your bodymind is clouded by illusion, you see only your own limitations.

8 **BODY and MIND:** Elevated levels of openness and personal optimism are both a part of and a result of Taoist practices.

9 **HEART:** The image of a laughing Taoist is a perennial Chinese archetype.

10–11 **BODY and MIND:** Accessing the intuition so the soul can take the lead in your life is the single most important aspect of your survival. At the same time, it must be balanced by an equal amount of "having a sense of humor about its importance." It is simultaneously vital and trivial.

12 **HEART:** If you do not have a sense of humor about yourself and your philosophy, then you cannot be a Taoist.

13 **BODY and MIND:** The wisdom-thread referred to in this stanza is an oral text that predates Taoism but became an important part of its genesis. These are truly ancient Chinese concepts.

14–27 **HAND, BODY, and MIND:** Stanzas 14 through 27 are a series of life questions that must be answered by the Cultivator. Each question is a conundrum that must be approached mystically to be solved. Solving them requires an investment of human energy sustained over months, even years. This becomes an important period of spiritual work for the Cultivator.

28–29 BODY and MIND: An injunction not to be in a hurry to solve the conundrums. It is the experience of the journey and not the destination that is important.

30–31 HEART: Western thought regards practice as something that must be difficult and endured before one can arrive at a point of completion or success. Practice is often regarded as something that we do to get ready for the "real thing." Taoists regard every moment in space and time as "the performance" and not "the rehearsal." How will you perform? According to your gifts and deficits. Nothing could be more perfect.

32–33 BODY and MIND: This is another spiritual conundrum to be mystically solved.

34 HEART: The Tao Source and life is the property of any and everyone. Cultivating it uplifts the entire world.

CHAPTER FORTY-TWO

1   living the *tao* way of life creates resonance
    and a life that is lived

2   resonance possessed of its own momentum creates
            difference
    difference possessed of its own momentum creates
    heaven
    man
    earth

3   the union of these three produces everything in the
            universe
    in a continuous wave
    that can be embraced and ridden
    by obliquely drifting within it

4   the ancient child asks
    how can you drift with the universal

5   by precisely blending my bodymind's lifeforce

6   the ancient child asks
    what must be blended to drift with the universal

7   body must blend with mind
    mind must blend with will
    will must blend with lifeforce
    lifeforce must blend with spirit
    spirit must blend with engaged movement
    engaged movement must blend with the void

8   the void is a doorway that sits at the center
    of the universe

9   the ancient child asks
    where is the doorway

10 between the beats of my heart
    between the inbreath and the outbreath
    between the beats of a drum
    between the decision and the initiation
    between my intention and my action
    between the words on this page

11 drift and fly
    by standing still
    feeling the continuity
    of the universe

12 there is nothing to worry about
    no matter where life takes you
    you are not alone and
    you never have been

13 sometimes drift more and sometimes less
sometimes stop and look around
sometimes briskly fly from peak to peak

14 an authentic journey cannot be forced

15 it unfolds with jostles and bumps
it sways to and fro

16 this is the only way to live

COMMENTARY

1–2 BODY and MIND: The Taoist concept of resonance refers to an alignment that can best be described musically. Imagine a room filled with tuning forks of different keys. The Tao Source vibrates in the key of C. The Cultivator arranges his life to vibrate at that frequency and the two become, in the parlance of science, a resonant system. The more entrained they become (i.e., support one another), the broader the vibrations become. These broader vibrations create overtones that, eventually, manifest all of the other keys of tuning forks in the room, increasing the resonant system. Soon, the entire room is vibrating harmoniously.

3 HAND: This is a specific cultivation technique in which the Taoist Cultivator strikes a specific meditative posture, adjusts his mental state, opens up to the resonant system of the Tao, and floats within it; that is, he gets lost in it.

4–5 HAND: A specific arrangement of the life-force energy facilitates the technique of Taoist flight.

6–7 HAND and MIND: A specific cultivation formula. Taoists refer to this as the Six Combinations:
a. Physical movement that is supported and motivated by specific mentation,
b. Mentation that is supported and motivated by imagination,
c. Imagination that is supported and motivated by mobilized *qi* energy,
d. *Qi* energy that is supported and motivated by spiritual consciousness,
e. Spiritual consciousness that supports and directs physical movement that radically alters the Cultivator's experience of consensus reality,
f. Transformative physical movement that appears, to the Cultivator, to be directed by the Tao Source itself. The physical movement alters the consciousness further.

8 HAND and MIND: When the Six Combinations have been achieved, the Cultivator is said to be "drifting in the Great Void." This is also called The Great Achievement.

9–10 **HEART and MIND:** Other ways of saying this might be: "It is the space between the notes that makes the music," or "It is the space between the bars that keeps the tiger in the cage."

11 **HAND:** These are specific instructions.

12–16 **HAND and BODY:** These are meditative instructions, as well as a model for living.

CHAPTER FORTY-THREE

1 the most soft and ethereal things of the world
   will always easily penetrate the hard and unyielding

2 those things that are without form
   will always penetrate the impervious structure

3 because the true heart of hardness is
   soft

4 because the true heart of impervious solidity is
   formlessness

5 the artist cannot paint a picture of water without
   showing its source or
   showing its destination

6 water will always wear down a stone

7 when I see water naturally seeking its own resting
        place
   I know that it will arrive at that point
   no matter what gets placed in the way

8 flow naturally like water
   without contention or coercion

and you will arrive at your destination
and resting place

9 few understand the wisdom of unforced non-action
because it cannot be expressed with words and
labels
it can only be intuitively felt

10 it can only be understood with the softness and
formlessness
of water

11 it can only be implemented with the softness and
formlessness
of water

COMMENTARY

1 **HEART:** This is a poetic exposition of the Taoist
concept of non-being through non-coercion, or *wu wei*.
Wu wei forms the basis of Taoist conduct. On the
surface, it enjoins the Taoist to avoid forcing and
controlling life. Gently suggesting yourself into life and
allowing it to unfold naturally is the Taoist way. Yielding
to its force, experiencing it completely, matching its ups
and downs, and resting peacefully with its rhythm and
flow forms the majority of the Cultivator's work.

2-4 HEART: The Taoist is formless and can, therefore, penetrate to the core of any phenomena, which is born from formlessness.

5 HAND and BODY: This is a reference to mystic calligraphy that informs Taoist conduct and behavior.

6 HAND and HEART: That which is formless is superior to that which has definite form. Water Wearing Down A Stone is a Taoist meditation technique that enables the Cultivator to penetrate to the root of individual thoughts. This technique found its way into the Ch'an Buddhist tradition and greatly influenced its mind-science.

7 HEART: Flowing water is a perennial Taoist archetype. A typical Taoist saying is, "Water is Heaven's way of teaching man to follow the Tao Path back to the Tao Source."

8 BODY, MIND, and HAND: Cultivators use flowing water as a model for the full range of human endeavors, including art, science, communication, movement, and governance.

9-11 HEART: Unforced non-action is another way of saying *wu wei*. Again, the formlessness of water is presented as the way to actualizing it.

♋ ✛ ♋

CHAPTER FORTY-FOUR

1 what is more important to you
what others think of you or
what you think of your body, mind, and spirit

2 is your natural energy, essence, and inspiration
worth more to you than acquired material things

3 is gaining
more or less
painful than losing

4 speaking with the mystery
refining your nature
studying your emotions
will inform you

5 if you love well
you will spend yourself well

6 if you love too often
you will exhaust yourself and die

7   when the power of the *tao* source of life
    flows into you from above
    contentment and happiness abound

8   when you know how to extend your love and life
    in a way that does not impose itself on the
        universe
    then you will flow into it
    knowing when to move forward and backward
    when to twist left or right
    when it's time to float upward or settle downward
    when it's best to move on
    or simply stand still

9   know these things and you will realize your
        limitlessness

10 be the sacred friend that joins the hands
    of heaven and earth
    accepting all the flaws and faults
    within and without your bodymind
    bearing on your shoulders
    the good and the bad all around you

11 and you will preserve the bodymind of the world

COMMENTARY

1 **MIND and BODY:** This refers to your self-image. Traditionally, Taoists cultivate a strong sense of self.

2 **MIND and BODY:** An alternate translation might be:
> your life-force energy, your vitality for living, and your soul
>
> are these worth more to you than earthly possessions?

3 **MIND and BODY:** Taoists often speak of "reaping the rewards of investing in loss." Said another way, we are in a constant state of losing and gaining simultaneously. We merely have to get out of the way of the process.

4 **HAND:** In this case, "refining your nature" refers to the practice of Taoist Alchemic Transformation. Essentially, the *qi* of your internal organs is balanced with the *qi* of your emotions, bringing profound order to your inner world. Thus ordered, the Cultivator has greater access to the Tao Source.

5-6 MIND and BODY: This is a call to emotional self-discipline. It also refers to the physical act of love, as well as our emotional commitment to our loved ones.

7 MIND and HAND: This is the natural order, which leads to genuine contentment.

8 BODY: Treat the world around you and those in it with great respect. These are instructions in the Taoist way of being.

9 BODY and MIND: Intuitively and respectfully interacting with those around you is the way to understand limitlessness.

10-11 HEART, BODY, and MIND: These stanzas outline the idea of Taoist social conscience.

CHAPTER FORTY-FIVE

1   sit quietly

2   focus and forget

3   rest within the great achievement

4   the ancient child asks
    what is the great achievement

5   it is beyond description in any language
    it can only be felt intuitively
    it can only be expressed intuitively
    engage a loose, alert, and aware
    body, mind, and sound
    then look into the formless
    and perceive no thing

6   see yourself as a sphere
    small at first
    growing to encompass
    the vastness of infinite space

7   sit quietly
    focus and forget then

in a state of ease and rest
secure the truth of the great achievement

8 employing the truth will not exhaust its power
when it seems exhausted it is really abundant
and while human art will die at the hands of utility
the great achievement is beyond being useful

9 great straightness is curved and crooked
great intelligence is raw and silly
great words are simple and naturally awkward

10 engaged movement drives out the frozen cold
mindful stillness subdues the frenzied heart

11 sit quietly
focusing
forgetting
summon order from the void
that guides the ordering of the universe

COMMENTARY

1–3 **HAND:** These are meditation instructions. The
Great Achievement, or *da cheng*, is a specific level of
accomplishment in Taoist cultivation.

4–7 HAND: Specifically, the Great Achievement begins as a free and unrestricted flow of *qi* energy throughout the bodymind. As this free and unrestricted flow of life-force energy increases, the bodymind is elevated to deeper levels of perception and awareness. Blocked *qi* results from employing too much mental or physical strength. When the *qi* is blocked or congested, it suppresses intention. Suppressed intention disrupts and disturbs the spirit, which, in turn, leads to physical and mental dis-ease [*sic*]. The meditation and *qigong* activities presented in this chapter remedy this situation.

8 MIND: This refers to the truth of cultivating the Great Achievement.

9 HEART: These are fundamental Taoist concepts.

10–11 HAND: Once the Cultivator succeeds in manifesting the Great Achievement, his spiritual state must be tested and refined through a series of specific physical movements. During these movements, the Cultivator maintains a perfect state of quiescence. As a result of exploring the outer environment with these movements, the Cultivator plunges deeper into his own interior environment. Soon, it feels as if the movements take on a life of their own directed by the Tao Source.

CHAPTER FORTY-SIX

1   when the powers and strengths of heaven
float downward into the earth
through man
the *tao* way of life presents itself
to everyone and everything

2   horses trained by men behave naturally and
       spontaneously
without any need for direction or control
their beneficence unfolds naturally

3   but when the powers and strengths of heaven
are blocked from flowing into the earth
man becomes isolated
and inoffensive creatures become warlike
multiplying in great numbers
and profaning the sacred
as the *tao* way of life recedes

4   the ancient child asks
what then presents itself

5   dissatisfaction with one's own essential nature
    dissatisfaction with one's own gifts and deficits
    dissatisfaction with the very ground one stands on

6   the worst thing you can do is to
    extend and reach into the world
    from a place of scarcity instead of abundance

7   one is restful
    the other is restless

8   the restless place is an unnatural field
    sown with discontentment

9   the restful place is an inexhaustible sacred precinct
    that goes where you go
    providing everything you need
    in just the right amounts

10 secure the restful place
    allow the power and strength of heaven
    to flow downward
    through you
    to the earth
    and quietly watch
    the *tao* way of life present itself
    to everyone and everything
    through you

COMMENTARY

1 HEART and MIND: The Tao Source is constantly blessing, granting, giving, and providing mankind with an overflowing abundance. When a person acknowledges this fact, the Tao Way of Living reveals itself.

2 HEART and MIND: This is a portrait of the Taoist Cultivator. The wild part of mankind is not tamed through cultivation techniques. Instead, innate human wildness is trained so that it can act according to its natural instincts. What results, Taoists believe, is an evolved human being that channels and overflows abundant beneficence to the world around him. Specifically, the power and strength of Heaven should be allowed to flow into the bodymind through the crown of the head.

3–5 MIND: This explains what occurs when people will not cultivate the Tao. When the Tao Source, manifesting itself through the power and strength of Heaven, is not allowed to flow into the bodymind, dissatisfaction results.

6 MIND: To live life in a state of "I'll never have enough" or "There isn't enough to go around" is to deny the Tao and retard your growth, as well as the growth of all mankind.

7–8 MIND and HAND: A restful state of being manifests abundance. A restless state of being manifests scarcity.

9 HEART: There is no shortage in Heaven. Once it is invoked, it will provide whatever you need.

10 HAND: These are meditation instructions. It is a way to place your self in alignment with the Tao Source and manifest the Tao Way of Life.

CHAPTER FORTY-SEVEN

1   the ancient child asks
      what is authentic knowledge

2   only revealed knowledge is authentic knowledge
      it flows from the heart's center
      within our way of living

3   the ancient child asks
      what is the heart center within our way of living

4   at the center of my own heart
      wherever I may be

5   alive

6   to know the world is not
      to think into it by reason

7   reason is not revelation

8   to know the world is
      to allow the world
      to think into you

9   wherever it may be

10 authentic knowing is revealed
    in a soul and to a soul
    seeking its lost home
    and resting place
    within deep regions
    of a centered heart spirit

11 the mysteries of the world
    come to you in a living light
    that breathes as you breathe
    infused with your own thoughts
    yet outlined as some distant place
    or thing

12 you may bring discipline to your knowing
    but you cannot bend it or shape it
    because it is already perfectly formed

13 you may know the world completely and
    understand its workings
    without ever leaving home

14 the ancient child asked
    what are the impediments to authentic knowing

15 wrong error is the first
    conquered by quiet sitting

16 wrong flight is the second
   conquered by flying obliquely with ease

17 wrong meditation is the third
   conquered by contemplative ritual

18 wrong purification is the fourth
   conquered by openness within a sacred precinct

19 wrongly embracing the doubt and despair of
       others as they are
   conquered by a humble appreciation of yourself
       as you are

20 the *tao* way of life bestows knowledge
   of all things under heaven
   to those who can travel the entire world
   with one ordinary deliberate step

21 in a lush green forest

22 one step

COMMENTARY

1-2 **HEART and MIND:** Presents a case for the
mystical experience. Knowledge revealed during a

mystical experience has more weight than knowledge acquired within the constraints of consensus reality. Mystics typically experience peace, contentment, and love flowing out from their heart to the world around them.

3–5 HEART and MIND: Taoist mystics experience this out flowing of human energy as a partial sacrifice of their own life.

6–9 HEART and MIND: This is a fundamental Taoist precept, as well as a criticism of Confucians. The followers of Confucius believed that the universe should be dissected, categorized, and analyzed with arcane systems of mathematics and logic. Taoists didn't feel the need to do the math, relying instead on a direct and complete experience of the mysteries of the universe.

10 MIND: This refers to the soul of the universe, of which the human soul is a reflection.

11 MIND: This is a preview of the Taoist illumination experience.

12 MIND and HAND: See Stanza 2 in Chapter Forty-six. You are a child of the Tao Source. What could be more perfect?

13 HEART: You may explore the entire universe without ever opening your door and stepping out of your house. All that is required is the mystic experience. Only a universe that is experienced mystically will reveal authentic knowledge and wisdom.

14 **MIND:** Lists those things that can block the mystic experience and the authentic knowledge that comes from it. These stanzas also list the remedy for each impediment.

15 **MIND and BODY:** Knowing how to make mistakes and learn from them.

16 **HAND:** Knowing how to perform *qigong* and other cultivation techniques properly.

17 **HAND:** Meditation can become forced and contrived. Ritual reminds us of what is important when meditating.

18 **HAND and BODY:** Isolating yourself, controlling your diet too much, becoming unavailable to others, renunciations, vows of solitude and poverty as a means to acquire spiritual credit actually block your connection to the mystic experience.

19 **HAND and BODY:** Becoming too involved in the troubles and woes of others will, likewise, block the mystic experience. Self-acceptance and love of self remedy this situation.

20–22 **HAND and HEART:** These stanzas are both a cultivation technique and a Taoist metaphor. The one step—or any physical movement for that matter—is a mindful one taken in the throes of a mystic state of consciousness.

CHAPTER FORTY-EIGHT

1   this one ordinary deliberate step

2   takes you away from increase
takes you away from scholarship
takes you away from the material intellect

3   and makes you a relaxed wanderer
who knows more and more
by knowing less and less

4   the usual is used and loses
the unusual is experienced and gains

5   the world yields readily to suggestion

6   by swinging your bodymind open like a gate
you allow the world to enter
at the behest of your intention

7   enjoy the wonderwork
as your invited guests mingle within
fill their glasses
arrange introductions

and allow the moment to unfold
without any interference or commentary

8   wherever you wander

9   be the perfect host
    be happy to be there

COMMENTARY

1–2 BODY: A description of Taoist Mindful Walking
as a means of cultivation. Essentially, this is a moving
meditation. The various minute physical actions
required to take a step are treated with full attention
and equanimity. As the bodymind becomes distracted,
the Cultivator gently brings his attention back to
monitoring his walk. This kind of activity is said to
purify the consciousness and organize the bodymind.

3–4 BODY and MIND: An authentic life is an
unlearning process. The idea of a "relaxed wanderer"
implies a deep connection to the land and nature.

5 BODY and MIND: Suggesting life, rather than
making demands on it, helps the Taoist overcome

blockages and resistance to the Tao Source. Simply put, you cannot force the Tao Way of Life to manifest. You can, however, allow it to appear.

6 BODY and MIND: The bodymind must embrace the force and flow of life.

7–9 BODY and MIND: This stanza uses the image of a banquet to make the point of allowing things to unfold naturally. The banquet in question takes place within the bodymind of the Cultivator.

CHAPTER FORTY-NINE

1   a wise man does not think first and then act
when the *tao* way of life presents itself

2   thinking first stops the moment from unfolding

3   when a mystery appears
he experiences it as completely as he is able
drawing no conclusions about it

4   when his heart and mind are uplifted
he feels
that dreams are far more tangible
than waking truths

5   he treats every one and every thing
with equanimity

6   he declares
I hold the good and able
as good and able

7   I hold the bad and inept
as good and able

8   to hold them all
    as equal and excellent
    is to gain virtue
    exponentially

9   for one person or thing
    is not
    more or less
    important
    than any other
    person or thing

10 truth is truth
    lies are truth

11 experiencing life in this way
    trains the bodymind
    to be united
    with the virtuous way of experiencing life

12 you become peaceful and reserved
    drifting
    within the field of all possibilities

13 playing like a child

COMMENTARY

1–2 MIND and BODY: Spontaneous actions and reactions in the face of life as it unfolds before you will build wisdom and maturity. If you think first, then you'll miss it.

3 BODY: The mystery is experienced mystically. It is important to note that Taoist education is held to be an "unlearning process."

4 BODY and MIND: These are the effects of experiencing life mystically.

5–9 MIND, HAND, and BODY: One of the psychological effects of the mystic experience is a growing sense that no event in spacetime is more or less important than any other event in spacetime. Taoists also employ equanimity as a cultivation technique.

10 HEART: Even at the core of a lie, the truth remains.

11–13 BODY and MIND: Being spontaneous, mystically experiencing everyday happenings, regarding authentic education as an unlearning process and regarding all phenomena with equanimity brings a coherence to the entire bodymind that sets the stage for a profound awakening to the Tao Source.

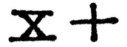

CHAPTER FIFTY

1   when the energy of heaven
    meets the energy of earth
    birth and death appear

2   between birth and death
    life appears

3   my bodymind opens to life
    nine ways
    my bodymind moves through life
    with four limbs

4   these thirteen parts together
    can move to create life or
    can move to create death

5   those who create death
    try to harden their life
    against it
    by forcing their life
    into still suits of armor

6 those who create life
  are impervious
  to claws and teeth
  to horns and blades
  to dangers above and below

7 the ancient child asks
  how can they do this

8 because they know how to
  step deliberately and move
  toward the creation of life

COMMENTARY

1-2 HEART: Speaks of the energy of birth and death as natural occurrences. Within the intermingling of the energy of birth and death, man appears. This is delivered by the Master in the direct transmission as if to say, "When the energies of birth and death intermingle, you the Cultivator appears."

3 BODY and MIND: "Nine ways" has multiple meanings, including:
a. The nine orifices of the body
b. Nine orbits of *qi* in the bodymind's energetic physiology

c. Nine *qigong* exercises that support cultivation
d. Nine stepping exercises that alter and focus the consciousness
e. Nine points of *qi* entry and exit on the body.

4 BODY and MIND: Physical movement that is designed to transform the Cultivator can cause harm if not approached properly. Also, how you arrange your everyday life can negatively affect your transformative movement.

5 HEART: Men who create death are men who are too rational. They indulge in thinking for its own sake and are beset by illusion.

6 HEART: Cultivators of the Tao Way of Life.

7–8 BODY, HEART, and HAND: In addition to being a Taoist core belief, it is also a metaphor for approaching life, as well as a specific *qigong* activity. The Cultivator, engaged in transformative movement, halts all physical motion in midstream, but continues to project movement via the intention. In other words, he physically stops moving but continues to see his bodymind moving.

CHAPTER FIFTY-ONE

1   the *tao* brings forth life
    the path and power of virtue nurtures that life

2   the spine of the world shapes them
    the mind of the world moves and completes them
    they are of a piece
    forming a harmonious unit

3   that is why a natural reverence
    for the *tao* way of life and its power
    manifests spontaneously

4   the *tao* way of life produces everything
    the way of virtue nourishes everything through
    birth
    growth
    maturation and
    death
    and acts as a protector and guide

5   mystic virtue assists but does not control
    as such it is mysterious to everyone
    and virtuous to all

6   the mystic knows
    that it is difficult to know
    which thoughts of *tao* making
    are his
    and which thoughts flow
    from the interplay
    of life and its nurturing

7   remember

8   the *tao* way of life
    allows

COMMENTARY

1-5 HEART: Cultivating the *Tao* engineers the
attainment of virtue, or *te*. The Tao Source flowing
from Heaven to Earth creates life of all different
kinds—all matter, the environment, "all that is." These
different kinds of life each has its own unique power
or virtue. All of these virtues are interconnected and
nourished by the existence of each other as intimate
expressions of the Tao Source. As such, they are as
profound and mysterious as the Tao Source. In
essence, Taoists regard virtues as pure expressions of

the Source on Earth. Cultivators seek to join deeply with the virtues of life as a means of achieving a deep connection with the Tao. This is called attaining Mystic Power or Mystic Virtue. Taoists believe that attaining Mystic Virtue is the most direct way to reclaim their most authentic and spontaneous self.

6–8 **MIND and HAND:** When cultivating Mystic Virtue, the Taoist Cultivator experiences a myriad of thoughts, visions, sensations, and emotions. Cultivators are encouraged not to attribute objective validity to any experience they have when cultivating Mystic Virtue. Instead, they are told to "let it happen" and to merely observe it dispassionately.

CHAPTER FIFTY-TWO

1 realizing the interplay of the *tao* way of life
and the virtue of nurturing all things under heaven
will introduce you to the primal mother

2 the mother of the world

3 resting peacefully with the mother
will introduce you to her sons and daughters

4 the sons and daughters of the world

5 these children can be exhausting
and though they mean no harm
trying to follow or control them
will only bring great danger to you

6 to be safe
rest peacefully with the mother

7 gently close your eyes
and look inward

8 softly direct your ears
to listen within

THE WHOLE HEART OF TAO

9 lightly close your mouth
raise your tongue to its roof
and quietly savor the interior

10 gently lift your crown
sit firm with a relaxed hold
on your bodymind

11 and let her love
fill you up

12 you will never be empty
again

13 remember
chasing children
brings calamity
no matter
how hard
you try
to follow
or grasp
them

14 the whole universe is in the palm
of your hand
but without
illumination
you cannot see it

15 the real world is not open
to the rational mind

16 the ancient child asks
when you have rested sufficiently
in the arms of the primal mother
and your vision begins to clear
what occurs

17 it is an unexpected sense of making
that first arises within the bodymind

18 then you are engulfed in a benevolent flame
that outlines rather than burns
and I do not know if I am
the source or the witness

19 the senses play
leaping to and fro
mischievously acting against their nature

20 emotions of comfort and satisfaction swell
so that even the harshest rain
feels like a lover's kiss

21 resting deeper
you feel as if an unseen enemy
has been vanquished
and life courses through your limbs
as the warrior's belt collects you

22 the connection to the *tao* source and way of life
    becomes punctuated and definite
    possessed of a wholly benevolent clarity

23 language leaves you
    and a light and sensitive energy collects at your
        crown

24 visions cascade upon you so rapidly
    that it becomes impossible
    to divide or discern
    what we normally regard as real

25 death becomes impossible

26 fire and force penetrate deeply
    within your bodymind
    and a new truth shapes you
    into someone altogether different

27 you begin to breathe
    the *tao* way of life
    as true respiration
    within a quickening
    that shines out
    for all to see

28 spinning out of the quickening
    you understand the mother's children
    you sing and dance

you paint and play
you look at the palm of your hand and

29 you see

30 you can still make mistakes
you can still be confused
you can still misstep
but you will always have the eyes of the *tao*

31 however
should you ever see yourself as separate from it

32 you will cease
to see
altogether

COMMENTARY

1–2 HEART: The ancient Chinese concept of the
Primal Mother is a complex one that predates Taoism.
As an integral part of the Taoist philosophy, it means
several things, including:

a. The field of *shen* and *qi* within the bodymind. This
is sometimes called the "lair of spirit and energy."

Each organ of the bodymind has its own unique spirit and energy.

b. A coherent and clear mystic state of consciousness in which the Cultivator palpably feels active non-action. Sometimes it is referred to as "the interplay of being and non-being."

c. A transitional or shifting state of consciousness often experienced as a meeting of two fields of image, thought, and energy that is sometimes called "The Yellow Valley of Non-Assertion of the Uncreated."

In the *Tao Te Ching*, all of these are referred to as the Mother of the World.

3–5 **HAND:** The sons and daughters are the various spirits and energies of the Cultivator's internal universe. When they are first experienced in meditation, cascades of sensation and mental images flood the bodymind. Some of these occurrences can greatly disturb the contemplative state of mind or even challenge the sanity of the Cultivator. Each event signals a mobilization of immense energy that has been produced during the ongoing process of Taoist cultivation.

6–10 **HAND:** These are specific methods for dealing with the cascades of sensation and image.

11–12 **HEART and HAND:** When the exhausting children are ignored, the entire bodymind is suffused with deep comfort.

13 MIND and HAND: This entire chapter lays the foundation for the practice of what would eventually become Taoist Alchemic Cultivation. Taoist Alchemy seeks deeper congress with the Tao Source by disciplining the sons and daughters of the Primal Mother. Various combinations and admixtures of the spirits and energies they represent are designed to accelerate the progress of the Cultivator. Many Taoist Alchemic methods have been developed over the centuries with some working better than others. Some of the methods are, in fact, very dangerous and should only be attempted under the guidance of a competent Taoist Master. Traditionally, none of these methods are required to successfully cultivate the Tao Way of Life.

14–15 HEART: These stanzas plainly state the need for mystic illumination.

16–32 HEART, HAND, and MIND: Illumination, or *ming*, is perhaps the most important event in the life of the Taoist Cultivator. Without it, total congress with the Tao Source cannot occur. During the direct transmission of the *Tao Te Ching*, the student either undergoes the illumination experience on the spot, or he must adequately describe his own illumination experience, which has already taken place. The rest of this chapter outlines the Taoist illumination experience. I have detailed it below in narrative form:
a. The onset of illumination is generally quite unexpected and takes the Cultivator completely by

surprise. Usually, one is engaged in cultivation practices, religious devotions, or some activity that is suggestive of the infinite within the finite.

b. Without any warning or indication whatsoever, the Cultivator instantly enters a belief system in which he feels he is engulfed in flame. Sometimes, one feels as if he is the flame itself. The force of this stage of illumination can be staggering. The Cultivator may lose his footing, stumble, or fall. Less dramatically, he may merely be rendered motionless while a faint cloud engulfs the bodymind. This cloud is associated with warmth, a flame, or a gentle fire that usually is red, purple, rose-colored, lavender, or reddish-orange in color. Some Cultivators experience the flame as coming from themselves.

c. Profound sensory shifts begin to take place. It's as if the senses are somehow briefly malfunctioning. Perceptual relationship begins to shift and change. Geometric shapes and images, usually seen only when the eyes are shut, present themselves to the visual field whether the eyes are open or not. These usually ectopic images are also more pronounced and startling to the Cultivator than what normally would be experienced.

d. While engulfed in the mystic flame and awash in what can only be described as sensory overload, the Cultivator begins to experience swells of emotion that can only be described as ecstatic. Profound comfort, deep satisfaction, joyousness, and an abiding sense of self-assurance are the most common.

e. Instantly following the emotional swells, the Cultivator feels as if he has silently conquered something, or has been quietly victorious over an unseen enemy.

f. Following the sense of being gently victorious, the Cultivator experiences a buildup of life-force energy around the belt line.

g. After the ascendancy of the silent and gentle victory, the Cultivator begins to gently touch the Tao. This contact is punctuated by the sense that there is no definite liberation from the planet—that he is already part of the Tao, as is all of creation. This realization of the Divine Force in everything persuades the Cultivator that the plan upon which the entire universe is constructed is completely adequate. There is no need to search for God; God is already here. Furthermore, this living Tao is viscerally experienced as being absolutely benevolent, giving, and ultimately good.

h. Instantly following the Taoist Sense of universal benevolence, the bodymind of the Cultivator begins to perceive—in a very palpable way—the holographic nature of the Tao, to wit, how all the parts of life are interconnected and interrelated to all the other parts of life. Concepts of space, time, and the like begin to break down altogether. Consensual reality becomes increasingly irrelevant as the Taoist sense begins to rearrange the words and pictures of the bodymind. For a time, it feels as if the faculty of language has exited from the Cultivator. Revealed visions then present themselves. These visions rapidly unfold as miniature dramas upon the bodymind of the Cultivator. The plots of these revealed plays are built upon archetypal themes, as well as on one's own life experience.

i. The Cultivator begins to believe in the literal impossibility of death, that an intimate relationship with the Tao has begun, that life and energy exist on other worlds and dimensions, that love and compassion are the natural order of things, and that happiness is humanity's birthright.

j. As the illumination further penetrates the bodymind of the Cultivator, conception, imagination, and the power of intellect expand. The Cultivator realizes the truth of thinking into rather than the facile thinking about something. Comprehension in the conventional sense slips away as a new way of thinking—global and intuitive in nature—inhabits the bodymind. Now, for the first time in this process, the Cultivator touches the truth that he has been fundamentally changed.

k. With the total realization that a permanent change has taken place, the Cultivator begins to feel, in Taoist mystical parlance, the "respiration of the Tao." The Cultivator, quite literally, feels as if he is glowing with the pulsating radiance of the cosmos.

l. This is a kind of spiritual quickening that, while nearing completion and at the end of the illumination experience, informs the Cultivator that, indeed, he must go through the fires again. In the Taoist tradition, there is not one single enlightenment, but many.

m. As the Cultivator exits the illumination experience itself, he will notice that he has increased intellectual capacity and a thirst for knowledge. He will be driven to create. If not previously ritualistic, an artist, or a musician, he will be drawn to ritual, music, and to art. He will exude a positive outlook on life and will examine facets of it as yet unexplored by him. The Cultivator will act in a more natural and spontaneous manner and will bring his added faculties to new projects and tasks. The world, to the Taoist Cultivator, will seem bigger, brighter, and more filled with wonder than ever before. An increase in communicativeness and overall charm will manifest. He will generate a personality that draws people to him.

n. Honoring this new outlook is perhaps the most important part of the illumination process. If the Cultivator mistakenly retreats inwardly and sees himself as separate from the world, then the chances of encountering another illumination decrease dramatically. If a fascination with mental or physical force, rampant emotion, personal power, isolation, or an unrestrained ego prevails, then the profound happiness will dissipate. In Taoist terms, the Cultivator will, spiritually, die.

o. Once Illumination has occurred, the lifestyle that the Cultivator has created along the way becomes vital in managing the elevated mystic experiences that naturally follow.

CHAPTER FIFTY-THREE

1 authentic knowledge is intuitive knowledge
  authentic knowledge is directly experienced

2 it is easy to enter the *tao* source and way of life
  through higher intuition

3 all you have to do is
  enter a sacred precinct
  pick up your life and bodymind
  adjust it to the moment in space and time
  play and create in the moment
  be happy and content with whatever occurs

4 revel with your creation
  rest with your creation
  rejoice with your creation

5 when timeworn ritual feels new
  you will see exactly where you are going
  and be able to walk the magnificent path
  in freedom measures
  slowly and deliberately

6 it is easy to get sidetracked and lost in the wilderness
it happens all the time
but
the worst thing you can do
is worry too much about it

7 smile
correct the course
bring yourself back to the great road and walk
slowly and deliberately

8 nothing else will solve the problem of getting lost

9 imposed order and rigid ritual are too clean
and won't produce anything of substance or
        beauty

10 magic coats with secret symbols cannot nullify
anger, violence, or confusion
at the center of a lost man

11 an authentic life cannot be stolen
false spirit is not the *tao* way of life

12 when order is imposed and ritual defiled
when anger, violence, and confusion are
        purposefully disguised
when you feed the stomach but not the soul
when you boast, brag, and push yourself on the
        world

13 you get further and further away from the *tao*
    source and way of life
indeed
you are its enemy

COMMENTARY

Taoist Masters will freely rearrange the chapter order during the direct transmission to fit the needs of the student and the occasion. Invariably, the stanzas in Chapter Fifty-three follow the exposition of illumination in the previous chapter. They serve as a reminder to the Cultivator that the illumination experience is the beginning of the mystic life and not the end. From this point on, the newly awakened Taoist must learn to "return to the Universal, follow the Eternal, and live like the Immortals."

1 **HEART:** This is a reminder to always experience life mystically.

2 **HEART:** Higher intuition is superior to reason and discipline.

3 **HAND and MIND:** These are instructions for actively engaging in "Tao Making."

CHAPTER FIFTY-THREE

4 MIND: This describes how you should feel about your process of Tao Making.

5 MIND and HAND: When the demands of everyday life take on a freshness and clarity, your intuition will mystically reveal the eventual results of your actions. "Walk[ing] … in freedom measures" has several meanings, including:
a. Mindfulness and deliberateness,
b. A mystic joining with the ordinary resulting in it becoming extraordinary,
c. A secret Taoist *qigong* activity.

6 MIND: Wilderness: the consensual world.

7–8 HAND: Be mindful and deliberate. Live life without hurries or worry.

9–10 MIND: This is a criticism of Confucius. Imposed rules of behavior, participating in grand rituals, wearing magic charms, and behaving according to societal dictates cannot change a man's heart.

11 MIND: "Stealing a life" means patterning your behavior after someone else. Each individual must find his or her own way.

12–13 BODY: These stanzas speak directly about the Grand Social functions of the time. Confucians believed that spiritual merit could be cultivated by engaging in polite behavior and standardized proper conduct at these functions. Taoists of the time believed that social occasions were actually warfare in disguise.

CHAPTER FIFTY-FOUR

1   to be firmly rooted in the *tao* way of life
    a bodymind must stand upright
    placing a portion of itself beneath the surface
    of the planet

2   standing naturally in this way
    enlivens the spirit
    preventing confusion and disturbance

3   the ancient child asks
    what are the watchwords for standing rooted in
        the *tao*

4   balanced   poised   equilibrium
    ease   relaxation   naturalness
    loose   playful   embrace

5   hold these nine and stand

6   you will not be shaken

7   your thoughts and their offspring
    will become ordered and finely tuned

possessed of an endless clarity
ritualistically conforming to the flux and flow of the
seasons

8 this is authenticity born of higher intuition
resting on the shoulders of one
truly alive

9 when a person holds the nine
he becomes genuine
influencing his family

10 when a family holds the nine
they manifest abundance
influencing their town and immediate locality

11 when a town and immediate locality hold the nine
they are filled with inner strength and wise force
influencing the entire country

12 when a country holds the nine
it extends its blessings worldwide
cultivating pervasive goodness everywhere

13 can you see it

14 a single person standing in the *tao* way of life
brings the life of the *tao* way to the world

15 for each of you

16 guided by higher intuition and taoist sight
identify every one you meet as part of your self
identify every thing you meet as part of your self

17 then you will see deeply
into the truth of your self
as you see deeply into the truth of others

COMMENTARY

1–2 HAND: This describes a *qigong* exercise. The Cultivator assumes a balanced standing posture, induces a state of quiescence, and places part of his *yi*, or mind, beneath the surface of the ground.

3–6 MIND and HAND: The Taoist Cultivator must bring these qualities to his practice of standing firmly rooted in the Tao.

7 MIND and HAND: This stanza describes the results of Taoist contemplative standing. Eventually, your organism becomes so sensitive that you can sense lunar and solar activity, as well as impending seasonal and climate changes.

8 BODY: A Genuine Life is one that is lived in accord with the natural flux, flow, and movements of the stars, planets, and the seasons. This profoundly affects the bodymind of the Cultivator and, by extension, the world around him. According to Taoist tradition, for example, individuals living a genuine life made the discoveries of Traditional Chinese Medicine, the compass, astronomy, gunpowder, binomial coefficients, and the seismograph, among others.

9 **MIND and HAND:** In this case, family refers to inner family of the Cultivator's bodymind—its spirits, energies, and internal organs.

10–12 **MIND and BODY:** A Cultivator of the *Tao* leading a Genuine Life manifests elevated levels of love, wisdom, wealth, and strength that overflows into the lives and community around him.

13 **MIND:** An alternate translation might be:
   is it possible to imagine such a wonderful chain of
      events?

14–15 **HEART:** This is a fundamental Taoist belief.

16–17 **HAND:** The spiritual exercise of seeing and reacting to everyone and everything you encounter as an extension of yourself is a powerful Taoist meditation into the truth of yourself and all of existence.

CHAPTER FIFTY-FIVE

1. vital essence
   a hand supporting your back

2. lifeforce energy
   a hand cradling your abdomen

3. human spirit
   a hand touching your heart

4. when these are balanced, poised, and equal
   you become spontaneous and full of life

5. when they are cultivated with ease, relaxation,
   and naturalness
   you resonate harmonically with the *tao*

6. when you stay loose and playful reaching out to
   embrace the world
   you become an invincible child impervious to harm

7. you will see

8   but if you allow them to compete
    with each other
    one of them will exhaust the other two
    and you will surely die young

9   what is dying
    dying is walking away
    from the *tao* way of life

COMMENTARY

1–3 HAND and MIND: During the direct transmission of the classic, the Master touches the student's bodymind as a way of focusing the student's attention on the specific "seat" of each of the Three Treasures:
a. The essence is experienced in the area of the kidneys,
b. The life-force is experienced in the *dantien*,
c. The spirit is experienced underneath the breastbone.

4–5 HAND and MIND: This refers to a dynamic balance of activity between the Three Treasures. When this dynamic balance is actively cultivated, you begin to contact the Tao Source.

6 **MIND and BODY:** Extend your powers into the world around you in a relaxed, understated, and innocent way.

7 **MIND:** You will mystically see into the true nature of all facets of life.

8 **MIND:** If the Three Treasures do not work in harmony, they can become disorganized and contentious. This spiritual contentiousness damages and drains the power of each causing physical, emotional, mental, and spiritual dis-eases [*sic*].

9 **HEART:** This stanza clearly defines spiritual death from a Taoist perspective.

CHAPTER FIFTY-SIX

1 anyone who really understands the *tao* way of life
finds living it easier than talking about it

2 anyone who really understands the *tao* way of life
finds that talking about it gets in the way of living it

3 children become noisy and unruly and they crave
attention

4 requiting dissonance involves diving into the earth
turning your senses inward
protecting your stores
unbinding your bodymind
tempering harsh glare and sharp edges

5 plunging deeply into the heart of the mystery
generates a wholeness for yourself
that is a wholeness of the world

6 at that point
the world honors you
because you honor the world

COMMENTARY

1 BODY and MIND: This is the paradox of Taoism. It is, fundamentally, a philosophy of action rather than conjecture. The truth is found in the doing and not in the thinking.

2–3 HEART: Man doesn't want to be a student. He would rather be a teacher. This is a natural outgrowth of the illusion of separateness and the first obstacle to the Taoist mystic life that must be breached. Becoming a Cultivator of the *Tao* means giving up preconceived ideas and personal opinions about it. In Taoist parlance, preconceived ideas and opinions are the unruly children. One must empty oneself of these ideas and opinions. The Cultivator must also give up the practice of arguing, analyzing, and discussing these ideas and opinions with others. If you do not, you are giving them attention they don't deserve and, subsequently, rewarding their bad behavior.

4 HAND: The noisy and unruly children create dissonance in the bodymind of the Cultivator. This situation is remedied by:

a. Mystically joining with the natural world,

b. Deeply attune your senses to the inner workings of the bodymind,

c. Passively observe the inner workings as if from a distance,

d. Unbinding has two meanings in this case:

    i. Deeply relax any perceived areas of tension or discomfort.

    ii. Balance any particularly unruly preconceived idea or opinion by seeing the other side of it. For example, (old idea) "I don't like that person. I don't think he's very nice or smart." (new idea) "Wait a minute; I could be wrong about him. I see some goodness. I should entertain the thought that he might be smarter and nicer than he appears."

e. Live your life under the influence of your new perception.

    This activity is a vital part of the Taoist unlearning process.

5–6 **MIND:** Unlearning results in a mystic completeness that engenders a profound sense of belonging and humbleness that deeply nourishes the bodymind of the Cultivator and everyone he comes in contact with.

CHAPTER FIFTY-SEVEN

1   think of yourself as an empire
to govern, explore, work, and live in

2   a man stretched between heaven and earth
governs the totality of the self
with ritual action and intent

3   a man stretched between heaven and earth
resolves conflicts within his borders
with surprise, creativity, and the unusual

4   a man stretched between heaven and earth
embraces the universe
by not interfering with it at all

5   it is a matter of degree
to see yourself as a ruler who governs
according to a definite plan
reacting creatively to the unexpected
while also
allowing your kingdom to unfold naturally

6   the ancient child asks
    where is this kingdom

7   the kingdom is within me
    within each of us

8   too many taxes
    too many laws
    and the kingdom will never be right

9   make just the precise amount of demands
    upon the kingdom of the self
    and you will be happy and abundant
    righted between heaven and earth

10 too many taxes
    too many laws
    and the kingdom will be in chaos
    it will act out of scarcity
    it will breed many thieves robbing their countrymen
    as the populace arms itself for survival
    for survival instead of living

11 the ancient child asks
    how do you remedy the situation

12 do things without appearing to do things
    act spontaneously within the limits of the moment
    touch the kingdom with a gentle hand
    embrace peace and cultivate stillness

shape your intention and let it overflow
allow good things to happen without meddling
allow your bodymind to order itself

13 cultivate for the sheer joy of cultivation alone

14 stretch yourself between heaven and earth
mindfully chip away at your life
to see
what is inside

15 do everything
by
doing nothing

COMMENTARY

1 **BODY and MIND:** The meaning is plain. Throughout the *Tao Te Ching*, the metaphor of government is used to describe the individual. Much has been written about Lao-tzu's fascination and disgust with the politics of his era. Unfortunately, most translators over-emphasize those aspects and neglect the central Taoist theme. From an ancient Taoist perspective, an individual who embraces the Tao Way of Life naturally influences the people,

community, and political institutions around him through a type of spiritual osmosis. By practical extension, techniques for an individual cultivation of the *Tao* are equally effective when applied to a kingdom or country.

2–4 BODY and MIND: The first lines of these three stanzas reinforce the idea that the Cultivator as ruler must act from a deep connection to the Tao Source if his governance is to be successful.

5 MIND: "Your kingdom" refers to the internal kingdom of the Cultivator's bodymind. It must be regulated according to a definite yet flexible plan and with deference to the mysteries of the human organism.

6–7 MIND: The inner world.

8–9 HAND and MIND: You must avoid exerting excessive control over and making too many demands upon the bodymind. To find just the right amount, the Cultivator must be guided by his intuition and be under full influence of the Tao Source.

10 BODY and MIND: Acting from a chaotic and confused place disrupts the various energies and spirits of the bodymind, causing them to work against each other. For example, wallowing in depression drains the *qi* of the lungs. Faced with a deficient amount of life-force energy to perform its function, the lungs steal *qi* from the kidneys. This starts a cascade of energy scavenging that soon negatively impacts the entire bodymind.

11–15 BODY and HAND: Beyond a gentle discipline, allow your life to unfold as naturally as possible. Live for the joy of living and allow happiness, abundance, and contentment into every facet of your existence. Complete your acquired knowledge by the unlearning method described in the previous chapter. Treat yourself as an uncarved block of wood. Chip away at yourself through cultivation and you will uncover your true self.

CHAPTER FIFTY-EIGHT

1   govern yourself with a light and sensitive energy
of hand, heart, and intent
and you will behave as one unified being

2   govern yourself without a light and sensitive energy
gently holding your heart behind a gate
and you will never be unified
as you pry and intrude upon yourself
becoming a collection of decaying parts

3   happiness
misery

4   the seed of one is always within
the other

5   they both come from heaven
they both fold one on the other
they both hide from each other
they both surprise each other
they both speak to each other
in a private language only they understand

6 this is the interplay of yin and yang
   you cannot stop or control it

7 seeing things as separate brings illusion and
      calamity

8 conform and shape yourself
   to the interplay of the yin and yang

9 discipline and order yourself
   like a great square without sharp edges or corners

10 train and integrate yourself in order
   to cut through confusion and illusion

11 without hurting yourself or others

12 it is difficult to illuminate without blinding

13 that is why the sage wise man strives for the
      authentic
   and not the artificial

COMMENTARY

1 HEART and BODY: Cultivating the *Tao* entails unifying the entire bodymind. This definition of wholeness also extends to the unity of man and the Tao Source. Taoist wholeness is achieved, in part, by gently negotiating a central place poised between the actions of the physical body, emotions, and consciousness.

2 HEART and BODY: If a point of central equilibrium cannot be established between those actions and maintained, the Cultivator and his life become scattered, dull, and confused.

3 HEART: A unified being experiences life as happy and joyful, while an un-unified being experiences life as dark, joyless, and miserable.

4 HEART: At the center of the movement between pairs of opposites is the central transition point that is common to both. This shared point is the "seed" in Taoism.

5 MIND: The extremes in each pair of opposites are perfectly natural and forever intertwined. Their seemingly contradictory natures are actually the result of their intimate relation with each other. They appear separate, but in reality, they are joined.

6 **HEART:** The constant oscillation of opposing forces in the universe began when the energy of the heavens met the energy of the earth. The interplay of these forces began the *yin yang* pulse of the universe. The vibrating pulse of *yin yang* interplay supplied the motive force of all creation. This spinning oscillation is eternal and beyond your ability to change.

7 **HEART:** Seeing all of creation as un-unified and outside the *yin yang* pulse harms the Taoist and all those around him.

8 **BODY:** These are specific *qigong* instructions. The Cultivator enters a quiescent state and physically moves his bodymind in the shape of the *yin* and *yang* known as the Great Ultimate Diagram or *T'ai Chi Tu*. Moving in this pattern brings the bodymind closer to the mysteries that the symbol represents.

9–10 **MIND:** This is a Taoist image that means employing a global perspective that sees the totality of any person, place, situation, or idea. Taoists believe that when you look at the totality of life, an illuminated mind will perceive far more similarities than differences. When you behave from this place, you are "ordering and disciplining yourself like the great square." Mystically understanding these shared points organizes and uplifts your life. It also accelerates your progress in cultivating the Tao Source.

11–13 **MIND:** Even the Taoist Mystic can become confused and overwhelmed by his constant and ever deepening experience of the Tao Source and Way of Life. Living an authentic life insures that he will not stray from the path.

CHAPTER FIFTY-NINE

1   if you want to bring
    order, peace, and prosperity
    to yourself
    then use a light hand and be gentle
    with yourself

2   establish a routine and stick to it
    step through the nine palaces
    patterning yourself after nature

3   cultivate in the early morning hours
    stand like a tree
    accumulating power, strength, and virtue

4   master all your treasures under the heavens
    sit like a mountain
    purifying your mind and consciousness

5   fortify your talents
    recline like a great river
    flowing throughout the land, towns, and
        countryside

6   collect your knowledge and wisdom
crawl on your hands and knees
penetrating deeply into the earth
awakening to your own endurance and potential
learn to appreciate your limits and you will be
      unlimited

7   release yourself to the *tao* way of life
roll firmly within the great mystery
absorbing the everlasting nourishment of living

8   create and play
become clairsentient
to the *tao* source of life
and you will become a boundless and everlasting
      immortal

COMMENTARY

Chapter Fifty-nine is considered by Taoist Cultivators to be a comprehensive description of qigong *exercises designed to harness the life-force energy of the bodymind. Mystic union with nature and the forces of the universe is experienced energetically, that is, in a field of* qi *that engulfs the Cultivator. Learning to channel and manipulate this energy at the very least leads to robust health, mental acumen, and physical longevity. Advanced Taoist Cultivators enter a belief system in which they viscerally experience the timeless energy of creation. When the Cultivator lives his life under the constant influence of this experience, he is said to be an Immortal, or* Hsien.

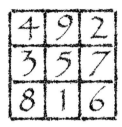

1 HAND: Approach all of these yogic activities in a relaxed and understated manner. Absolve yourself of the need to be successful in your *qigong* endeavors. The journey is more important than the destination.

2 HAND: Your *qigong* practice should be part of a daily ritual that becomes the most important part of your day. The "nine palaces" refers to a ritualized stepping pattern. The Cultivator imagines that employing this mystic dance grants him greater access to Nature and the *qi* of the Universal. The Nine Palaces dance is usually performed out of doors in a beautiful natural setting.

3 HAND: *Qigong* practice should take place in the early morning hours when the *qi* and the air are fresh

and the bodymind is rested. Standing Like a Tree refers to the practice of standing meditation.
a. Assume a balanced and stable standing posture.
b. Imagine that you are drawing physical and spiritual sustenance from the earth.

4 **HAND:** Preserve and balance the energy, vitality, and spirit of the bodymind. Sit in meditation and imagine that you are like a mountain. In Taoist cosmology, mountains are expressions of vibrant earth energy that reach up to the heavens. They are, however, bound to the planet. Imagining yourself as a mountain clears your mental faculties and elevates your consciousness.

5 **HAND:** Engage in activity that is profoundly meaningful to you, such as art or music. "Reclin[ing] like a great river" refers to the practice of reclining *qigong*.
a. Lay on your side in a relaxed fetal position, preferably near a riverbank.
b. Imagine that you are that river or another great body of water flowing across the land. You imagine that you are seeking the lowest resting point possible.

6 **HAND:** These are instructions for crawling *qigong*.
a. "Collect your knowledge and wisdom" by focusing on your lower *dantien*.
b. Mindfully crawl on your hands and knees while attempting to absorb the *qi* of the earth into the front of your torso.

c. Pretend that each time you place your hand or knee on the ground, it penetrates deeply into the planet.
d. Convince yourself that you are a vast and inexhaustible being that could traverse the entire globe in this manner.

7 **HAND:** These are instructions for rolling *qigong*.
a. Stretch out on the ground and deeply relax.
b. See yourself sinking into the earth's surface as if your molecules are melting into the ground.
c. Slowly roll back and forth upon the ground. Don't move too quickly, but you should feel slightly disoriented.
d. As you roll, imagine that you are slowly working your way deeper into the planet.
e. With every inhalation, absorb the energy of the earth deeply into your bodymind.

8 **HAND:** Engage in a creative pursuit, such as dance, art, painting, poetry, etc. As you do, actively try to sense and feel the Tao Source creating through you as you relinquish creative control to it. Following these procedures will, according to Taoist cultivation, turn you into an Immortal.

CHAPTER SIXTY

1   it is important that you attend to great matters
as if they were small and delicate ones
or your inner and outer worlds will be uneasy
and confused

2   hands on
hands off

3   a nourishing meal requires
just enough presentation
and not
one bit
more

4   when the influence of the *tao* source of life
exists itself through many cultivators
across the land
evil has less impact or potential

5   the ancient child asks
how is this possible

6   because a sage wise man evenly stretched
     between heaven and earth
     coaxes his soul from within and
     allows it to take the lead
     in his life

7   no ghost
     demons or
     tormentors
     can hurt him
     inner or outer

8   soon his balanced benevolence overflows
     to everyone and everything
     around him

9   and the influence of the *tao* source of life
     envelopes and protects the world under heaven
     allowing its original nature
     to present itself

COMMENTARY

1–3 MIND and BODY: The first three stanzas of this chapter are presented to the student during the direct transmission as a kind of graphic conundrum. The Master paints a series of characters in random order and arrangement on a single piece of paper. The student is asked to "read between the lines" to decipher the meaning. The presented translation conveys the desired response. Alternate translations might be:

treat large projects just like small ones
or,
govern a large country as if you were cooking a small fish

This is a pre-Taoist metaphor that means "Don't overdo."

4 HEART: The very existence of Taoist Cultivators in a community brings order, benevolence, and peace to that community.

5–8 HEART: Peace, benevolence, and order are the direct results of the Tao Source expressing itself through the soul of man. If this expression is allowed to influence everyday life, then spiritual strength and energy cause an ever-increasing spiritual momentum that uplifts everyone. This momentum protects the entire community and subtly urges everyone in it to seek a deeper connection to the Tao Source.

9 HEART: When you behave authentically and reclaim your childlike innocence, those around you catch a glimpse of their own innocence and the joy it brings. Another way of encapsulating the meaning of this chapter sums up Lao-tzu's concept of social conscience. To wit, "One person cultivating the *Tao* benefits everyone."

CHAPTER SIXTY-ONE

1   here is the formula
    for discovery
    of the original self

2   see yourself as a great river
    identify with the fountainhead in the mountains
    identify with the watercourse across the land
    identify with the emptying into the great sea

3   this is the receptive

4   rest peacefully within the shape of
    an empty vessel
    blanketing your bodymind with stillness

5   tranquil sitting
    balances the naturally expressive
    with the naturally receptive

6   see the great river within you
    see the great river beneath you
    see the great river above you
    see yourself as small within the great river

7　the great and the small have no meaning
　　on their own
　　because they are the same thing

8　they wish to serve each other

9　bring them together
　　as the river connects the mountain spring
　　to the vast ocean

10　and the original self
　　will appear

COMMENTARY

*It is important to understand that Taoists are more
concerned with the experience of being fully alive than
they are with finding meaning in life. As such, they
approach life in the spirit of exploration and discovery.
Whatever they discover is invariably experienced with
"radical amazement" and a reverence for the journey.
Engaging in this journey naturally brings them closer to
the Tao Source.*

*　Like the beginning of the previous chapter, the entirety
of Chapter Sixty-one is presented during the process of*

direct transmission as a series of mystic riddles involving social order, political influence, and the roles of men and women. In reality, this chapter is a proscribed method of intimate self-exploration designed to lead the Taoist Cultivator to his original self. The translation adequately reveals this technique.

1–3 HAND:

a. Imagine yourself as the totality of a great flowing river.

b. See the beginning of yourself as drops of melting snow on the highest mountain peaks.

c. Imagine the path that you cut through the land and all of the communities that cling to your banks for survival.

d. See yourself emptying into the ocean, becoming a small part of its vastness.

e. Continue mindfully cycling through these images and yield completely to them.

4 HAND:

As you achieve a state of quiescence, imagine that you are an empty vessel waiting to be filled up by the Tao Source. Generate a feeling of gentle anticipation.

5 HAND:

As much as you are able, embody peace and tranquility. You should sit in a stable meditative posture while being as still as possible. This will balance the receptive *qi* with the creative *qi* of your bodymind.

6 **HAND:** The instructions are plainly stated in the translation. Fill your mind with these images.

7–8 **HEART:** Opposites are dependent upon each other. When they work in harmony with each other, the entire world benefits. Cooperation is their natural state, not opposition.

9–10 **HAND:** Taoist archaic language refers to this activity in several ways, including unifying the energy of opposites, blending the male with the female and balancing the creative with the receptive. Performing this technique draws out the original self.

CHAPTER SIXTY-TWO

1 manifesting the *tao* way of life
requires you to emulate the great river
under the heavens

2 and flow with the watercourse of seasons

3 surrendering to the natural ordering
brings you to the repository
of all knowledge and wisdom
that only the original mind
can see
or use

4 magic words will not gain you entrance
good deeds will only shape your intention
but will still not let you in

5 open your back and front
open the waist
open the arms and legs

6 play freely without judging
your gifts and your deficits

for your entire being
is a treasure

7 stretch upward with your crown
and see yourself
sitting peacefully and ordered

8 within the three
golden elixir fields of cinnabar
in their peaceful order

9 hold your heart gently
for it is a round jade disc
with a hole in the center

10 presented to the task at hand
as a great gift
offered to the *tao* source of life

11 move your arms and legs
restrained at the cliff
demonstrating your nobility, power, and inner
strength

12 hold your symbol of the *tao* source of life
high above your head
as if holding a hammer that will never fall

13 and the vast and mysterious repository
will open and flow
into you

COMMENTARY

1–2 MIND and HAND: It is not unusual for ancient Chinese to be preoccupied with the image of a great river. For good and ill, the Chinese experience was historically greatly influenced by rivers that not only provided an abundance of food and commerce, but also regularly overflowed their banks with devastating results. Learning when it was safe to be near the rivers and when it was best to be far away from them was an ancient and essential survival skill. Surrendering to the natural flux and flow of the river for physical survival became a metaphor for spiritual survival as well.

3 MIND and HAND: Surrendering to the flux and flow of the Tao Way of Life yields great wisdom that can only be understood by the authentic, innocent mind.

4–6 MIND and HAND: Taoists know that the beneficence and love extended by the Tao Source are the only real securities in life. Good works, spiritual trappings, and complex rituals are not sufficient to allow that love and beneficence into your life. You must open up to the totality of the Tao Source.

Furthermore, you must use your essence, energy, and spirit to experience it as completely as possible.

7 **HAND:** This is a technique for surrendering to the Tao Source.

8 **HAND:** Imagine that the three *dantien*s are aligned one over the other.

9–10 **HAND:** Strive to not be overwhelmed emotionally as the Tao Source flows through you. Jade is an archaic image for the essence of expressiveness. The hole in the middle of it is the symbol for receptiveness. Together they represent abundance through a balancing of the creative and receptive energies of the Tao. The Cultivator sees his heart as the essence of this abundance that he offers as a sacrifice of human spirit to the Tao Source.

11 **HAND:** Engage in Transformative Movement as a means of refining and managing the mystic experience.

12–13 **HAND:** Imagine that the spinning and oscillating forces of the universe are coalescing above your head, sending pulsating waves of energy down through your bodymind. Eventually, you will perceive a small opening in space appearing over your bodymind, as well as a downward flow of mystic energies.

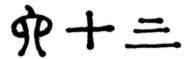

CHAPTER SIXTY-THREE

1 act decisively by actively
  being still and appearing
  to do no thing

2 hear what others will not hear
  taste what others will not taste
  touch what others will not touch
  smell what others will not smell
  feel what others will not feel
  think what others will not think

3 reach into the small and make it large
  touch the multitudes and with a turn of your wrist
  make them few

4 know the virtue of turning your palm
  from covering the earth
  to supporting the heavens
  and those things that are wrong within and without
  will be righted

5 attend the moment
  at the moment
  do not wait until the task is half over

6 being one degree askew in the beginning
results in missing your destination altogether
and no matter how well planned a journey is
there will always be a need for course corrections

7 in fact
sage wise men will not even think about a
    destination

8 before their journey
begins
they have already
arrived

9 if you make a promise to yourself
keep it

10 not going to your heart spirit
forces it to come to you
in disorder
that disturbs the bodymind
crippling it to living

11 approach everything with respect for the magic
inside of it
adhering to the terms of each encounter
so life will unfold
easily

COMMENTARY

1 BODY: This is an injunction to the Taoist to lead a mystic life. It invokes the ideas of being by not-being, doing by not-doing, and active non-action that forms the Taoist mystics' stock in trade.

2 BODY: Experience all things mystically and in a non-ordinary manner.

3 MIND and BODY: This means that you should mystically project yourself into everyone and everything you encounter. It is also a reminder to regard everyone and everything you meet as being a part of yourself.

4 MIND and BODY: The Taoist Mystic has the power to be the steward of the heavens and the earth. As such, he is able to care for it by continuously cultivating a Taoist lifestyle.

5 BODY: Attend to life as it presents itself. Act spontaneously and immediately as needed.

6 **BODY:** Make adjustments as they become necessary. The only constant in life is change. Be ready for it and behave accordingly.

7–8 **MIND:** We learn by doing and not by arriving. Do not force any situation into a preconceived outcome. You will complete the journey before it begins by surrendering to the journey and allowing it to teach you what it will.

9 **MIND:** Respect your own divinity and basic goodness. Treat yourself well.

10 **HEART:** Listen to your heart and ask the soul to lead the journey. If you don't ask your heart and soul for advice on your life's journey, you are forcing them to get your attention any way they can. This is frequently unpleasant.

11 **HEART:** Look for the action of the Tao Source in every person or situation you meet.

CHAPTER SIXTY-FOUR

1   that which is

2   balanced   poised   equal

3   will be peaceful and at rest
     amidst the flow

4   the key is your spirit and its management

5   the ancient child asks
     how do you manage your spirit

6   embrace active non-action effortlessly
     balance yin and yang within your bodymind
     poise your will, thought, and imagination
     equalize your lifeforce and be under its influence
     believe in yourself but never compete
     wear your spirit like a radiant mantle
     surrender to the deep pleasure of individual
        attention

7   remember
     building nine palaces can begin

with a single earthen brick
held in your hand
if you give it your undivided attention

8   ten is real
ten times ten is genuine
ten times ten times ten is pure

9   steps taken in an authentic journey
possessed of breadth and depth
must rise up from the earth
to meet your feet
which take each step as if it were
the first
and only
step
you will ever take

10 never try
only do

11 and then
use your spirit to communicate

12 project the pleasurable depth of your spirit
outward
extending authenticity and simple pride
to all

13 experience your self as intimately connected
   to all
   awakening a unified bodymind response
   at just the right moment
   in space and time

14 it is much easier for the *tao* to believe in you
   if you believe in yourself

COMMENTARY

1–4 **HAND:** You can bring these three qualities to any
encounter or situation. The Taoist Cultivator extends
and infuses ever-increasing levels of balance, poise,
and equilibrium into life events as an exercise in
shengong, or spirit building.

5 **MIND:** Manage in this case means to strengthen
and refine.

6 **HAND and BODY:** This stanza lists the ways to
build and manage your spirit:
a. Do not force your spirit; do not work at it or try too
hard.
b. Yield to the oscillating waves of *yin* and *yang*;

maintain a constant awareness of the inner flux and flow; maintain an equal amount of expressiveness and receptiveness in your bodymind.

c. Activate the will, thought, and imagination getting them ready to act spontaneously and naturally.

d. Activate and balance the *qi* energy throughout your bodymind.

e. Hold a simple mystic pride; accept your talents and accomplishments with a self-effacing reverence; do not force yourself on the consensual world or the people in it.

f. Smile; project great happiness and joy; present yourself to the world in a truly happy state that sparkles with peace and contentment.

g. When dealing with a person, give them your complete and undivided attention. Treat places and events in the same manner.

7 **MIND:** The largest accomplishment begins with a single small accomplishment.

8 **MIND:** This is a Taoist mystic reference that implies, among other things, an exponential growth of spirit that begins with the simplest spiritual attainment.

9 **HEART and BODY:** This describes how you feel when your *shen* is being cultivated.

a. You react spontaneously and naturally.

b. You become intensely mindful of whatever you are doing; you merge with the object of your attention.

c. It feels as though the earth's energy raises up to support your physical actions.

d. Each movement you make feels like the first movement you have ever made. They are complete and whole.

10 HAND and BODY: Expect nothing and be open to anything.

11–13 HAND and BODY: Employ your *shen* as you move through your daily activities. The translation is specific. Also, your spirit will grow and strengthen at its own pace. Your soul will make you aware of this growth at precisely the right time. Expect nothing and be open to anything.

14 MIND: To visualize the Tao Source in this way helps manage your contemplative experience during *shengong*.

CHAPTER SIXTY-FIVE

1   men of excellent virtue during ancient times
were very skilled in cultivating
the *tao* way of life
but knew the dangers of understanding
something
too quickly

2   unsophisticated people will speculate
beyond what they intrinsically know
and draw conclusions
false and firm

3   combating the false and firm
requires humor and astonishment

4   it becomes difficult to harmonize the bodymind
when you think
that you know it all

5   cleverness traps the bodymind
certitude robs the bodymind

6   outer knowledge
must reconcile with
inner knowledge

7   those who understand these two
allow distance to measure itself
instead of measuring distance
because directly experiencing
mystic virtue
requires turning inward and reconciling
your inner life
your outer life

8 harmonizing the seen with the unseen

COMMENTARY

1 **MIND:** "Man of excellent virtue" is an archaic Taoist term applying to an individual who "follows the rules of the universe, absorbs the essence of the sun and the moon, aligns his mind with the movement of the stars and planets, is intimate with the changes of the seasons, embodies the workings of the *yin* and *yang*, and is able to foresee their movements." This forms the primary definition of a Taoist Cultivator.

2 MIND: Cultivators do not rush to judgment. Quickly attributing any objective validity to any mystic experience you have is dangerous. Speculating about spiritual experiences too soon after their occurrence leads you to draw false conclusions about it.

3 MIND: Unsophisticated people, in Taoist terms, are unhappy people. Sophistication or happiness is essential for living a spiritual life. Unsophisticated people experience life with preconceived notions and think that the key to happiness is like finding the missing piece to a puzzle. Cultivators know that happiness is self-created with a relaxed countenance and a sense of radical amazement about life.

4–5 MIND: You cannot successfully cultivate the *Tao* if you grasp and cling to your preconceived notions about things. Absolve yourself of the need to be the smartest person in the room and give up the need to be right.

6–8 HEART: True happiness is achieved when you actively transform an ordinary experience into a spiritual one. The Taoist reality is that you are not as separated from the spiritual side of life as you think. Reclaiming this notion and allowing it to manifest in your day-to-day life begins by listening to the dictates of your soul.

CHAPTER SIXTY-SIX

1   the ancient child asks
how do you access this great harmony

2   by becoming a long river flowing downward into
      the sea
of consciousness, mind, and will
seeking the lowly resting point
slowly along the way
not compressed by earthen dams
but naturally guided to the sea

3   the ancient child asks
how should you stand and speak to the world
      around you

4   with a portion of myself
within the earth
as nourishing root and length
more in it than above it

5   the ancient child asks
how should you lead the world around you

6 by example
   without trying to control the common details of
        living

7 contending causes contention
   have no part of it

COMMENTARY

1 **HAND:** The great harmony is the cumulative activity of turning ordinary activities into spiritual ones.

2 **HAND:** This is a description of the meditative technique that supports the great harmony. It is also a model of the process. Simply put, you should slowly flow into the ordinary activity as if seeking a resting point deep within it. Let the activity tell you how much vigor you should use during the merging.

3–4 **HAND and BODY:** Stand in a balanced posture outdoors. Imagine that you are standing deep within the earth and not merely on its surface. This meditative technique fortifies the energy of the great harmony.

5–7 **MIND and BODY:** The Cultivator who is happy and resonates happiness will make others happy, too.

Any desire to exert control over the process of being happy destroys it altogether. Appreciate what naturally occurs and learn to let go of the need to decide how happiness presents itself.

CHAPTER SIXTY-SEVEN

1   stand in the shape of greatness
    with feet resting firmly upon the land
    and arms ringed as if holding a large tree
    embracing and holding the vastness
    of the *tao* source of life

2   it seems silly that such a simple activity
    can bring you to greatness
    but it can

3   in fact
    if it didn't appear silly and simple
    it would not be worth it
    at all

4   stand in the shape of greatness
    radiating a mother's love for all the world
    restraining the outflowing of your lifeforce
    remaining vigilant and aware of the world's
        momentum

5   for a mother's love is selfless and fearless
    restrained lifeforce is amplified until needed

and vigilance will help you avoid the knives
that are all around you

6   for true greatness to present itself
moderation is the key

7   being too compassionate in your life
being too generous with your life
being the leader who saves everyone else's life
will end your own
before its time

8   a mother's love is an impenetrable fortress
a mother's love is an unstoppable weapon

9   stand in the shape of greatness
with a mother's love
and heaven will flow into you

COMMENTARY

1 **HAND:** "Stand[ing] in the shape of greatness"
means several things:
a. The stanza adequately describes the physicality
and the intent of the meditative posture.
b. Normal human happiness usually relies on clinging
to past memories that we associate with being happy.

However, to be truly happy, the Taoist must let go of his accepted notions about happiness. "Stand[ing] in the shape of greatness" means giving up your attachment to past and current sources of happiness and making yourself a fit receptacle for some new source to come in.

2–3 MIND: The simplest approaches are the best. Complex methods are neither productive nor useful.

4–5 HAND: Assume the "shape of greatness" and radiate love and compassion to everyone and everything around you. While the love and compassion radiated outward should flow unrestricted, your *qi* should only be extended sparingly. Attempt to be completely and totally aware of your immediate surroundings.

6 HAND and MIND: Practice this meditation gently; take it easy.

7 HEART and BODY: This stanza advocates moderation when helping others. Sacrificing yourself for the sake of others is not a Taoist virtue. Eventually, it will destroy your spirit.

8 MIND: The mother referred to in this stanza is the Primal Mother.

9 HAND: Cultivating the "shape of greatness" allows the Tao Source to flow into your bodymind.

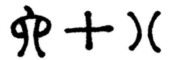

CHAPTER SIXTY-EIGHT

1   a true warrior is not deliberately belligerent
and does not show off his fighting skills

2   a true warrior is a gentle man
and does not lose his temper

3   a true warrior is not entangled in the trivial
and does not need to win arguments

4   a true warrior
does not look or act like
a true warrior

5   but he is a true warrior
possessed of an ancient virtue
that is non-contentious and sublime

6   under heaven
he knows how to unite himself
with heaven
peacefully complying with the principles
of heaven

7   a true warrior
stands firm

COMMENTARY

This entire chapter uses the image of a warrior to describe the Cultivator of the Tao. The true Taoist Warrior is a spiritual warrior that enters the mystic with confidence, bravery, and resoluteness.

1 **BODY:** "Fighting skills" in this case refers to mystic skills.

2 **BODY:** The true Taoist Warrior is naturally gentle and not prone to violent outbursts.

3 **BODY:** Minutia is not important to the Taoist Warrior. He doesn't need to be the most important and most intelligent person in a gathering of men.

4 **BODY:** A Taoist Warrior doesn't look like an ordinary fighting man.

5 **BODY:** A Taoist Warrior preserves and protects an ancient code of ethics and conduct.

6 **BODY:** A true Taoist Warrior practices cultivation.

7 BODY and HEART: This line reflects the classical Taoist image of a brave and forthright warrior. He is, indeed, a champion of the Tao Way of Life.

CHAPTER SIXTY-NINE

1   it is difficult to understand the need
for a warrior under heaven
but conflict is a fact of life
that lies at the heart of conflict's absence

2   peace

3   so you must behave like a warrior
when a warrior is needed

4   the ancient child asks
how do you behave like a warrior

5   act as a defender and not as an invader
march forward without appearing to march forward
be lazy about tying up your war coat
utilize a war hand only as needed
use your empty hand before drawing a sword
be measured and resolute in battle
even though you would rather abstain

6   the greatest harm you can do is to
treat your opponent lightly

7 give him his due and win the day
   or you will lose touch with your inner world

8 when two opposing forces meet
   and do combat
   the one that is compassionate and yielding
   will surely conquer
   the other

COMMENTARY

1 HEART and MIND: This describes the need for a
spiritual warrior. Each Taoist must, at some point,
identify with and become a warrior. This emotional
stance builds the resoluteness, discipline, and
determination needed to deeply penetrate the Taoist
mysteries. The Taoist Warrior does battle with those
physical, psychological, intellectual, and spiritual
enemies that would stop him from profoundly
cultivating the Tao.

2 HEART and MIND: That peace resides at the core of
aggression. The seed of *yin* resides at the center of *yang*.

3 MIND: A warrior's behavior is based on an unflinching and unwavering respect for both the enemy and the task of meeting him in battle.

4 BODY and MIND: During the direct transmission of the Classic, this question is put to the student with great seriousness. He is expected to answer quickly and with great poetic clarity.

5 BODY and MIND: The guidelines for behaving like a warrior are multifaceted. They are practically applied in both the presence and the absence of an enemy.
a. Gather your assets. Prepare and refine them. Be constantly alert and ready for action. When the enemy presents himself, resolutely move out to join him in battle. Regard his territory with great respect, for you are securing it for those who live there.
b. Make adaptable plans and be prepared to project your forces anywhere even when no enemy presents himself.
c. When an enemy presents himself and it is clear that you must fight, deliberately move to battle in an unhurried and unworried manner.
d. Do not deploy the full strength of your assets too soon.
e. Use only as much force as is necessary to fully accomplish the task at hand.
f. Pick your targets and define your goals. Make sure that they are realistic. Design your battle plans for complete success and execute them with verve and confidence.

g. Boundless and unfocused aggression is not the way of the warrior. It is to be avoided. However, the precise amount of focused aggression applied at just the right moment invigorates the land and benefits everyone.

6 **BODY and MIND:** A lack of aggression and resoluteness toward your enemy fundamentally disrespects your relationship to him. The warrior must fight to win. Anything other than complete and total victory further interrupts the connection to the Tao Source. This interruption guarantees the reemergence of the enemy at some later date.

7 **BODY and MIND:** The goal of your enemy is your destruction. He wishes to sever your connection to the Tao Source. He cares not for the disruption he causes by bringing war to you. If you deal with him lightly— or not all—his chaotic energy will infect your country and eventually destroy it.

8 **HEART:** A warrior understands the relationship between himself and the enemy. He knows that behaving with a lack of aggression shows a fundamental disrespect for the parties and dynamics of the situation. Though he does not universally advocate or condone violence, when forced to protect himself, the warrior does so with great resolve and determination. But even as he prevails, the true warrior holds a quiet remorse at the center of his

victory. It is this appreciation for the realities of combat—spiritual or otherwise—that assures his victory.

CHAPTER SEVENTY

1 the ancient child asks
can you keep my teachings
everything I am saying to you
both my words and what they teach
are very easy to understand and put into practice
yet so few people on this planet
are able to do so

2 the ancient child says
complicating my teachings will turn them to nothing

3 the ancient child commands
speak for me

4 my words and what they teach are a time-binding
    song
with ancient roots and an infinite length

5 my corporeal actions reveal a time-bound method
that seeks to keep me aligned with the universe

6 my words and my actions are so oblique
that logical attempts at understanding me are futile

7 knowing   me   not   me   knowing

8 know me by not knowing me
   and I become clear and rare to you

9 know me by not knowing me
   and I will appear elegant and sacred to you

10 know me by not knowing me
   and I will open my precious heart to you

COMMENTARY

This point in the direct transmission of the Tao Te Ching *signals a watershed moment for the Taoist initiate. Until now, the Master has been regarded as the primary source speaking for Lao-tzu. Beginning with the fourth stanza of this chapter, the student becomes the conduit and speaks for the Ancient Child. Within the constraints of the classic itself and the ritual moment, the Master hangs back and silently observes the student as he composes verse, expresses it in brush and ink, and recites it aloud.*

1-2 **MIND:** Consensus reality relies on intellectual reasoning, a reliance on preconceived notions and rationalization for support. Taoist reality relies on intuitive reasoning, the challenging of preconceptions and a direct experience of life. A practical application of Taoist principles that is conducted in the spirit of exploration is fundamentally incompatible with rationalization. Simply put, you must do it and not think about doing it. Trying to figure out and intellectually understand the Taoist Path without actually walking it only leads to unnecessarily complex and incorrect assumptions about the Tao Source and Way of Life.

3 **HEART:** The Master turns over the responsibility for channeling Lao-tzu to the student.

4 **HEART:** The total message that is the 5,000 Character Classic of the Ancient Child is a constant signal that forms the Tao Source, which infinitely stretches backwards and forwards in time.

5 **HEART:** The ancient cultivation methods that allow one to traverse the Tao Path are creations and embodiments of the constant signal flowing from the Tao Source to mankind.

6 **HEART:** You cannot know my behavior by comparing me to other behaviors.

7 **HEART:** This is the fundamental Taoist injunction.

8–10 MIND: Lao-tzu, speaking through the initiate, reveals the results of "knowing by not-knowing." Lao-tzu speaks as an embodiment of the Tao Source.

CHAPTER SEVENTY-ONE

1 knowing by not knowing is an unconscious
     understanding
  that exists subtly as transcendent and lofty

2 it is revealed knowledge
  that flows with ease from within

3 all the knowledge of the universe can be sensed
  at the corner of your senses
  locked away inside each and every cell of your
     bodymind

4 getting to it requires
  that you flow with ease from within

5 trying to understand the subtle and transcendent
  consciously
  will put you in a state of
  dis-ease
  blocking the flow from within

COMMENTARY

This chapter continues the recitation of fundamental Taoist principles by the student. This recitation will continue well into Chapter Seventy-four. During this process, the Master remains silent as he draws more than 200 esoteric Chinese characters in small random groups for the student to copy and interpret. These are furious bursts of calligraphic call and response that intensify the mystic experience of direct transmission. Both Master and student, to quote Dante, become "transhumanized."

1 **MIND:** Taoist knowledge and understanding, which are difficult to describe, are acquired by searching the finite for the infinite.

2 **MIND:** Taoist understanding can only be attained through intuition.

3 **MIND:** The wisdom, knowledge, and secrets of the universe are already locked away inside your bodymind. You just have to unlock it.

4 MIND: Unlocking the transcendental wisdom and knowledge requires the cultivation of natural, balanced, and gentle methods of introspection.

5 HEART: Employing the direct methods of the conscious mind to investigate the *Tao* will interfere with your connection to the Tao Source of Life. Ultimately, mental, physical, and spiritual sickness will result.

CHAPTER SEVENTY-TWO

1   treat yourself with respect as you cultivate the *tao*
         way of life

2   authentic wisdom as revealed knowledge
     can become overpowering and make you afraid
     because its implications are profound and far-
         reaching

3   the force of revealed knowledge
     can sometimes make you feel small and insignificant
     push you to austerity and
     make you feel undeserving

4   the sage wise man is not afraid
     and is content to be overpowered

5   know that you are vast and significant
     deserving of all the good things that life has to offer
     and life will always be at your fingertips

COMMENTARY

1 MIND and BODY: This is a very important concept. Even in Lao-tzu's time, many people engaged in self-negating spiritual pursuits that focused on the inherent evil in men and the corruption and hardships of normal existence. Taoism, the antithesis of that thinking, saw mankind as naturally divine and day-to-day existence as a continuing opportunity to more fully realize that divinity. It follows then that man, inherently good, should live life with joy and gusto.

2-5 MIND: Because we are unaccustomed to listening to it, we can become unsettled when the soul speaks to us. Invariably, it tells us that to gain new ground we must give up the comfort of preconceptions. Yet, we must learn to invest in loss and become comfortable with the idea. The Taoist Mystic learns to enjoy the poverty of illusion because he knows that as an expression of the Tao Source if he gives up what he has, he is only making room for something more wondrous to come in. Indeed, wonder is his birthright.

CHAPTER SEVENTY-THREE

1   do not be reckless with your life
    blind courage and blind passion can kill you
    however
    courage and passion informed by revealed
        knowledge
    can fill you with abundant lifeforce

2   one is for life
    one is for death

3   the force of heaven flowing with ease
    through a bodymind cultivating the *tao* way of life
    overcomes any obstacle and sustains that
        bodymind

4   the force of heaven flowing with ease
    speaks without words and answers questions
    before they are complete

5   the force of heaven flowing with ease
    can be summoned by only a gentle invitation
    and a door left open

6 the force of heaven flowing with ease
   appears spontaneous while
   acting according to a divine plan

7 the force of heaven flowing with ease
   through a bodymind cultivating the *tao* way of life
   appears unhurried and unworried
   peaceful and delicate

8 its comings and goings are blessings
   that are beyond your control

9 heaven's net is a gossamer web covering the world
   connecting every single thing under it
   to every other single thing under it

10 think of things in this way
   and you will become
   the force of heaven flowing with ease

COMMENTARY

*The student's exposition of Taoist principles continues.
His poetic recitation, physical countenance, and quality
of life-force form the basis for judging his level of mystic
engagement and accomplishment.*

1 **MIND and BODY:** Temper yourself with intuitive knowledge and awareness.

2 **MIND and BODY:** Courage and passion that is not guided by your soul will ultimately hurt you.

3 **HEART:** Cultivating the *Tao* heals and nourishes the bodymind of the Cultivator.

4 **MIND:** The intuitive mind knows precisely what you require at every moment. It knows this even before you do. It communicates to you in feelings, sensations, and mental images.

5 **HEART and MIND:** You cannot compel the wonders of the Tao to attend you. You must ask gently and respectfully without any attachment to the outcome.

6 **HEART:** The Tao that appears both spontaneous and planned is the true Tao.

7 **BODY:** This stanza describes the outward appearance and behavior of a Cultivator of the Tao Source.

8 **HEART:** The Tao Source is constantly sanctifying and purifying us.

9 **HEART:** Every particle of existence is part of every other particle of existence. We are all connected to one

another. We are all connected to every single thing in the universe. Everyone you meet is, in reality, your self.

10 MIND: Regarding every one and every thing that you encounter as being a reflection of yourself fundamentally alters your consciousness. In this altered state, you will experience a state of unobstructed communion with the Tao Source.

♆ + ♋

CHAPTER SEVENTY-FOUR

1 if you believe in the literal impossibility of death
   you will not fear dying
   and life will always be available to you

2 if you fear death
   you will become fearful of life
   and
   complicated situations
   perverse thinking
   bizarre events
   dishonest behavior and
   deceitful people
   will bind your hands and be at your throat

3 the ancient child asks
   who are the bodymind killers

4 complicated situations
   perverse thinking
   bizarre events
   dishonest behavior
   deceitful people

5   these things drain away your lifeforce
     causing accidents and injury
     to every one around you
     no matter how able and resilient you may be

COMMENTARY

1 **MIND:** As a part of the everlasting Tao Source, you are everlasting. Said another way, you are a spiritual being brought into existence to experience a human life. When your human life naturally ends, you will return to the Tao Source as a spiritual being.

2–4 **MIND:** In Taoist terms, the fear of death is expressed in many different and interesting ways. In this case, it refers to living a full and complete life within the bounds of human frailty. The physical realities of disease, health, happiness, sadness, and the causes of pain and pleasure are mysteries of the human organism. If you become preoccupied with how these mysteries play out, you will gravitate toward the complicated, perverse, bizarre, dishonest, and deceitful.

5 **HEART and MIND:** The final stanza is clear. When you allow the complicated, perverse, bizarre, dishonest, and deceitful into your life, all sorts of

calamities and mishaps follow. In Taoist archaic language, the "bodymind killer" is nothing less than a master executioner. No matter how rational, optimistic, or strong you may be, the executioner's ax will surely fall and diminish your life.

CHAPTER SEVENTY-FIVE

1   requiting the bodymind killers
takes too much energy
and starves you for living

2   a starving bodymind rebels and acts unruly

3   knowing it cannot easily die
it makes you sick, heavy, and anxious
attempting to grab your attention
entreating you to listen to its cries

4   a living bodymind asks you to get out of its way
and let it live

COMMENTARY

1 BODY and MIND: The time and energy you spend to mitigate the damage left in the wake of the bodymind killers is vital time and energy that you should've spent caring for yourself. No merit is gained when you sacrifice yourself in this manner.

2-3 BODY and MIND: As soon as you indulge the complicated, perverse, bizarre, dishonest, and deceitful, your soul tries its best to warn you. If you do not listen to it speak through your intuition, the soul will look for other ways to get your attention. This can include causing you discomfort and pain, confusion and forgetfulness, or sickness and disease.

4 BODY and MIND: Your soul wants to take the lead in your life. You have but to let it.

CHAPTER SEVENTY-SIX

1   the ancient child asks
    how do you get out of the bodymind's way and
        let it live

2   by allowing your soul to take the lead of your life

3   the ancient child asks
    how do you let the soul take the lead of your life

4   be as gentle and tender as a newborn
    soft, yielding, supple, and full of lifeforce

5   avoid stiffness, rigidity, and naked force

6   emulate the living things of the world delicately
    and at a distance

7   avoid hardening your bodymind and spirit
    avoid those unyielding things that stink of decay

8   embody those things that are tender and pliant
    which grant life and freedom

9 avoid mustering your talents and collecting your
strengths
in a forceful or headstrong manner

10 remember
an unyielding tree will snap under a strong wind
or fall easily under a dull ax

11 pattern yourself after a great tree
with deep roots and strong branches
and you will exalt your bodymind and spirit

COMMENTARY

1-3 **BODY and HEART:** Your bodymind, bathed in
the Tao Source, wants you to get out of its way so it
can be truly alive. This is accomplished by letting your
shen, or soul, guide you.

4 **BODY and HAND:** Bring these qualities to all
facets of your life.

5 **BODY and MIND:** Taoists refer to stiffness, rigidity,
and force as mystic litter or spiritual debris that
impedes the Tao Way of Life.

6 BODY and HAND: Make nothing that isn't patterned after nature or cannot be touched by it.

7-8 BODY and MIND: This is a call to mimic those things in nature that are vibrant and robust. The qualities of young growing plants and animals, lush forests, flowing rivers, flocks of birds, and even the movement of the winds and the clouds are the primary sources of inspiration for the Taoist.

9-10 BODY and MIND: Abruptly gathering yourself physically and mentally hardens your bodymind and spirit. Ultimately, this hardness steals your ability to react appropriately to changes in your inner and outer worlds.

11 HAND: These are specific instructions for standing meditation.

ᵾ + ᵾ

CHAPTER SEVENTY-SEVEN

1 bend the bow and embrace the tiger
   to emulate the way of heaven

2 drawn with resoluteness
   the bow changes length and width
   turning in on itself

3 released with resoluteness
   the bow projects its arrow fixedly to a target
   by equalizing itself

4 the bow can shoot up or down as needed
   always seeking to balance out
   flexibility and cohesion
   always seeking to resolve
   excesses of energy and deficiencies of energy

5 equalizing and balancing out and resolving
   are the ways of heaven

6 but the ways of man
   make things unequal

imbalanced and unresolved
cutting man off from heaven and earth

7   only a sage wise man humbly cultivating the *tao*
        way of life
    can entreat heaven on man's behalf
    asking heaven
    to reestablish the natural order
    by not asking heaven

8   when he is successful
    he does not dwell on it
    displaying his skill at emulating the way of heaven

9   he simply smiles
    and moves on to the next task

COMMENTARY

1-4 HEART and BODY: These stanzas ask you to
emulate the qualities of a bow and to do so with the
tenacity of a tiger. The description of the drawing a
bow and releasing an arrow form a complete formula
for living the Tao Way of Life.

5 HEART: The Taoist emulates the way of Heaven by bringing balance and resolution to his life and the life around him.

6 BODY: Non-Cultivators who do not intrinsically understand the Tao Way of Life invariably bring imbalance to all that they think and do. Eventually, the momentum of this imbalance grows until it negatively infects anyone that is around them. Over time, this negative momentum radiates outward to infect not only their family, but also their city, state, and beyond.

7 BODY: The Taoist Cultivator can intercede and help reestablish the natural order. They accomplish this by their own example and the actual practice of Taoist cultivation.

8-9 BODY: The Cultivator is humble, reserved, and understated. When he is able to reestablish the natural order, he relaxes deeply, blesses the world around him, and quietly moves on to where he is needed. Much Chinese folklore centers on the wandering Taoist Mystic who brings his skills and sensitivities to those he meets during his journeys.

CHAPTER SEVENTY-EIGHT

1 remember
   to be at your best
   pattern yourself after water

2 nothing in all the world is softer or more powerful
   nothing in all the world can substitute for it
   nothing in all the world can stop it

3 in their hearts
   everyone easily knows that
   the soft and weak
   will always overcome the hard and strong
   but they find it difficult to live this way

4 the secret is to
   move the bodymind like water

COMMENTARY

At this point in the direct transmission of the Classic, the Master employs changes in tone and syntax, as well as other devices that suggest the beginning of a journey. This is to be a journey of actualization where the student, now fully initiated into the Taoist Mysteries, takes what he has learned and applies it to every facet of his life.

1-2 BODY and MIND: These stanzas remind the Cultivator to pattern his life and actions after flowing water. Ultimately, the divinity of water informs the life of the Taoist giving him both a model for living and an image that forms a comfortable refuge.

3 BODY and MIND: Another way of saying this might be, "Everyone knows that the meek shall inherit the earth but so few are willing to engage in behavior that might mistakenly signal weakness or vulnerability."

4 BODY, MIND, and HAND: Think fluidly, move and exercise like flowing water, and live life as if you were a great river flowing through it.

CHAPTER SEVENTY-NINE

1   harmonizing great resentments and injuries
    requires a soft but steady equilibrium

2   but even in a gentle balancing of the scales
    some friction and pain will always remain

3   harmony can still be reached
    if the sage wise man doesn't push
    for complete unity

4   the sage wise man comes to understand that
        flawless justice
    is impossible
    so he holds an even temperament instead

5   great knowledge comes from the left hand
    holding something broken and flawed

6   accept the small inequities

7   a bodymind embracing the *tao* way of life
    doesn't need perfection

a bodymind rejects the *tao* way of life
striving for perfection

8 remember
heaven lends its strength to those who
follow the natural laws of the universe

COMMENTARY

1 **BODY:** When helping others, be gentle and patient.

2 **BODY:** No matter how gentle and patient you are, however, the process can still be painful and difficult for all concerned.

3-4 **BODY:** Perfection is an affront to the Tao. Searching for it interferes with your connection to the Tao Source and severely limits your spiritual growth. Do not insist on perfection and be happy with essential correctness and dynamic balance.

5 **MIND:** Something that is essentially correct has more potential for unlocking the intuitive and spiritual than something that strives for perfection. Imperfection in our own selves is the supreme mystic opportunity.

6 MIND: Accept imperfection.

7-8 MIND and BODY: The meaning of the translation is plain, yet a paraphrase may clarify it even more. As children, we embraced the Tao and played with no sense of judgment or outcome, and we created our wonder-world of play freely. Unfortunately, as we grew older, others often told us that our play wasn't quite good enough. We became less free and our world became less wonderful. As a result, we rejected the Tao by limiting our sense of self and our playful endeavors. We cut ourselves off from the creative power of Heaven. To reclaim it and restore the natural order of life, we have but to freely play and create anew.

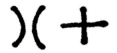

CHAPTER EIGHTY

1   keep your life simple and interesting

2   striving for great talent and skill
striving for great and perfect tools
is not the true way

3   have just enough talent
have just enough skill
have just the right amount of tools for work
have just the right amount of weapons for protection

4   the ancient child asks
how much is the right amount

5   know one hundred songs
so you can play a single simple melody
from the heart
to a heart

6   treat complex things
as simple things
arranged in a pattern
that

once you are at peace
can be easily deciphered

7 remember your ancient roots
read your history
relish your food
revel in your habits and customs
rest in your home
return to the tried and true

8 place great value in the natural order
of life and death

9 do not wander far from home

10 play and have fun in your life
and your backyard
will become a world
that will take you a lifetime to explore

11 what could be better

COMMENTARY

Most translations of the Tao Te Ching *tend to over-emphasize the military and political implications of*

Chapters Eighty and Eighty-one. After all, the Classic itself was written during a period of Chinese history called the Warring States Period. The culture of the time heavily emphasized martial virtue, as well as artistic and cultural pursuits of a more benevolent nature. A precise balance of the cultural and militaristic was thought vital to maintaining a thriving society. Therein lies the Taoist model for ideal living; a dynamic balance must be maintained so that one is not at war with oneself. The final two chapters describe how you should live in order to achieve and maintain this state of balance.

1 **BODY:** Simple: uncluttered, unconfused, direct, with clarity of purpose. Interesting: engaging, lively, challenging, with verve and joy.

2 **BODY:** "Striving" in this case, is born out of the mistaken notion that you simply are not good enough, smart enough, or talented enough to get the most out of your life. Taoist Cultivators believe that all the tools, secrets, and skills necessary for completely experiencing life to the fullest are locked away inside each and every cell of their bodymind. Cultivation is specifically designed to access those tools, secrets, and skills.

3 **MIND:** By way of example, having too much talent and skill in music can destroy your ability to, simply, enjoy the tune. You can have so many tools that you become mired in choosing the best one to complete a

task. You may have many weapons to protect yourself but, because of their great number, find yourself unable to employ any of them effectively. You can be so good at something that you lose your connection to your roots.

4-5 MIND and BODY: Ordinary living requires that you grow, learn, and mature. Authentic living takes place when a Cultivator, skilled in the workings of the Tao Source and Way of Life, expresses his unadorned natural self with childlike wonder and abandon.

6 BODY and MIND: Another way of saying this might be, "Complicated things are, in reality, groups of uncomplicated things that are formidably stacked one atop another. Look at seemingly complicated things in this way and they won't intimidate you."

7 MIND: You may become so successful at cultivating the *Tao* that you will lose your connection to your roots and your sense of self. Do not completely discard the trappings of the ordinary world and become austere. Everything and everyone that you've encountered in your life is an important part of you. If you turn your back on them, you are turning your back on yourself.

8 MIND: Death is as natural as life. It is an important part of the ground of being and experience. You should revere and honor both.

9 MIND: Stay close to your original self, keep to your routine, and do not take the ordinary for granted.

10 **BODY:** Live your life with the wonder and abandon of a child who plays for the sake of playing. If you are radically amazed by whatever you do or encounter along the way, the universe will open up and reveal her secrets.

11 **BODY:** Spiritual learning, growth, and evolution are impossible without divine play within the Tao Source. Divine play is the Taoist Cultivator's way of life.

)(+ −

CHAPTER EIGHTY-ONE

1   words that communicate success
   are not complex and showy

2   they are simple and direct

3   words that transform the bodymind
   are not adorned and fancy

4   they are plain and well-placed

5   words that speak of the *tao* source and way of life
   are open and few

6   words born of the union of perception and
          preception
   are not true words at all

7   true words are silent

8   the sage wise man does not live to accumulate
   instead
   he lives to help people
   because the sage wise man realizes that

how he behaves toward others
is really
how he behaves toward himself
and the universe

9 he is in harmony with the *tao* source and way of life

10 because
as man
he stands with outstretched bodymind and hands
between heaven
and earth

COMMENTARY

1 **BODY:** Taoist Cultivators are not boisterous and do
not brag about their accomplishments. They do not
engage in complicated arguments or try to persuade
you with elegant speeches. Rather than speak about
accomplishment or success, they simply make themselves
available to it.

2 **BODY:** For a Cultivator, the formula for a complete
experience of life is a simple and unambiguous one:
simply enter the Tao Source and live!

3-4 BODY: The translation is plain. Words that truly inspire are simple and common words delivered in the vernacular of the people. Ordinary words, spoken from a place of gratitude and humility, have the greatest ability to transform people and the lives they lead.

5-7 BODY: These three stanzas encapsulate the Taoist world view.

8-10 BODY: Taoist Cultivators live to appreciate the world and everyone in it. They are generous and helpful to others because they understand that all of us are connected to each other as expressions of the Tao Source. Realizing this fact and living his life accordingly, the Cultivator of the *Tao* becomes the steward and benefactor of the entire universe.

Notes:

Notes: